Crochet Totes and Accessories

Vice President and Chief Operations Officer: Tom Siebenmorgen
Vice President, Sales and Marketing: Pam Stebbins
Vice President, Operations: Jim Dittrich
Editor in Chief: Susan White Sullivan
Director of Designer Relations: Debra Nettles
Senior Art Director: Rhonda Shelby
Senior Prepress Director: Mark Hawkins

Produced for Leisure Arts, Inc. by Penn Publishing Ltd.
www.penn.co.il
Editor: Shoshana Brickman
Technical editing: Rita Greenfeder
Design and layout: Ariane Rybski
Photography by: Danya Weiner, Elan Penn page 80
Styling: Roni Chen

PRINTED IN THE U.S.A.

ISBN-13: 978-1-60140-871-6
ISBN-10: 1-60140-871-4
Library of Congress Control Number: 2009931659

Cover photography by Danya Weiner

Crochet Totes and Accessories

by

LENA MAIKON

A LEISURE ARTS PUBLICATION

contents

introduction

Looking for just the right purse to bring to the theater? Or maybe you'd like to make a crocheted tote for storing groceries when you stop at the local market. You'll find something to fit both of these occasions (plus many more!) in **Crochet Totes and Accessories**. This collection of bags, totes, purses, and sacs contains more than 20 crocheted projects that are attractive, distinct, and designed with a special purpose or occasion in mind.

For example, the Fashionably Striped "Fabric" Purse is just right for a day at the office; the Snowy Vintage Handbag is stylishly suitable for an evening at the theater. Bring along the Sun and Sea Beach Bag, with its plastic, easy-to-clean lining, the next time you go to the beach. Genie's Jewelry Box is perfect for storing your favorite jewelry, and the Brightly Striped Fringed Bottle Holder is ideal for slinging a water bottle over your shoulder on a hot day. There are projects for carrying textbooks to school, toting along pens and pencils, holding loose change, and much more.

While every project is distinct, several of them can be combined as sets. For example, you can treat yourself with a four-piece collection that contains a shoe bag, lingerie bag, make-up holder, and jewelry container, or a two-piece set made up of a beach tote and matching sunglass holder. You can also make complementary projects as special gifts for friends and relatives.

In addition to using yarns and fabrics that are pleasant to the touch, hemp fabric, hemp yarn, suede, and plastic mat lining are used in several projects, to emphasize textures and enhance durability. This is always important with handmade crocheted items, but especially important when the items are going to be held and clasped, opened and closed, carried on your back, draped over a shoulder, or wrapped around the waist. All of the projects are crocheted for maximum durability, so that they are sturdy enough to be used in your daily life.

You'll find a diverse range of colors used in these projects, from bright blues and yellows, to classic black and white, earthy greens and browns, and pretty oranges and pinks. That means there is something for every season, and to suit any style.

I hope that each time you flip through the book, you'll find something different that catches your eye, strikes your fancy, and sets you running for your crochet hook.

about the author

Lena Maikon learned to knit and crochet from her grandmother at the age of five in her hometown of Novosibrisk, Russia. She picked up the hobby again many years later, as a form of creative therapy. This quickly turned into a passion and profession. Lena, who often uses unconventional materials in her designs, dreams of creating a knitted and crocheted world. She crafts socks, shoes, dresses, handbags, flowers, vases, and light fixtures. She has published three creative knitting and crocheting books, and has her own handmade clothing and accessory label, Leninka. Lena is the mother of two young sons.

essentials

standard yarn weight system

Yarn Weight Symbol & Names	LACE 0	SUPER FINE 1	FINE 2	LIGHT 3	MEDIUM 4	BULKY 5	SUPER BULKY 6
Type of Yarns in Category	Fingering, size 10 crochet thread	Sock, Fingering, Baby	DK, Light Worsted	DK, Light Worsted	Worsted, Afghan, Aran	Chunky, Craft, Rug	Bulky, Roving

*GUIDELINES ONLY: The chart above reflects the most commonly used gauges and needle sizes for specific yarn categories.

** Lace weight yarns are usually knitted on larger needles to create lacy openwork patterns. Accordingly, a gauge range is difficult to determine. Always follow the gauge stated in your pattern.

CROCHET TERMINOLOGY

United States	International
slip stitch (slip st)	single crochet (sc)
single crochet (sc)	double crochet (dc)
half double crochet (hdc)	half treble crochet (htc)
double crochet (dc)	treble crochet (tr)
treble crochet (tr)	double treble crochet (dtr)
treble double crochet (dtr)	triple treble crochet (ttr)
triple treble crochet (tr tr)	quadruple treble crochet (qtr)
skip	miss

SKILL LEVELS

■□□□ Beginner	Projects for first-time crocheters using basic stitches. Minimal shaping.
■■□□ Easy	Projects using yarn with basic stitches, repetitive stitch patterns, simple color changes, and simple shaping and finishing.
■■■□ Intermediate	Projects using a variety of techniques, such as basic lace patterns or color patterns, mid-level shaping and finishing.
■■■■ Experienced	Projects with intricate stitch patterns, techniques and dimension, such as non-repeating patterns, multi-color techniques, fine threads, small hooks, detailed shaping and refined finishing.

CROCHET HOOKS

U.S.	B-0	C-2	D-3	E-4	F-5	G-6	H-7	I-9	J-10	K-10½	N	P	Q
METRIC - MM	2.25	2.75	3.25	3.5	3.75	4	5	5.5	6	6.5	9	10	15

Yarn selection

To make an exact replica of the photographed items, use the yarns listed in the Materials and Tools section of the projects. All of the yarns in these projects are readily available in the United States and Canada. Feel free to substitute them with yarns of your preference. Remember that with a different yarn, you'll need to adjust the crochet gauge to the measurements specified in the project instructions. Consider in advance whether you'll need to adjust the quantity of yarn for your project, especially if you're ordering the yarn online.

Gauge

Crochet a gauge swatch before beginning any project. If you want to obtain the exact results described, you must reach the gauge listed for that project. Try using different crochet hook sizes for the gauge, experimenting and measuring until your swatch contains the required number of stitches and rows. If you want fewer stitches per inch/ cm, use larger hooks; if you want more, use smaller hooks.

Even if the size of the project you crochet doesn't match the specified measurements, the instructions for finishing (cutting and affixing lining, attaching sides and straps, etc.) will still be applicable.

Don't be surprised that I often use hooks smaller than those recommended for a specific yarn. Though it may be more difficult to crochet with a smaller hook, I choose to do so deliberately to create a "fabric" that is durable and holds its shape.

materials and tools

Bias tape

Used to cover fabric edges and prevent fraying.

Buckles

Used to make closures for straps that have an adjustable length.

Buttons, snaps, zippers, and Velcro

Used to fasten some projects and add a decorative touch. Though the size and style are specified in each project, feel free to adjust as desired.

Chopsticks

Black lacquer decorated chopsticks are used as handles in the Rolled Sushi Purse.

Handles

Used to coomplete some projects. May be handmade or readymade.

Hemp rope and yarn

Used in several projects for crocheting and other purposes.

Hemp sack cloth

Used to make the body of the Decorated Shoe Sack.

Hemp straps

Used for straps and decoration.

Leather hole punch

Used to punch holes in plastic and suede pieces.

Parchment and tracing paper

Used to make templates.

Pencil

Used to copy templates.

Place markers

Used to mark places while working.

Plastic drawer mat

Used as a washable lining in the Sun and Sea Beach Bag.

Reversible lace fabric

Used for the lining of the Parisian Floral Purse. Since the lining extends above the top of the purse, both sides of the fabric are visible.

Scissors

Used in several projects to cut and trim various materials.

Sewing needle and thread

Used in several projects to sew on buttons, connect linings to bodies, and sew pieces together.

Straight pins

Used to hold pieces in place prior to sewing.

Suede pieces

Used in several projects to make and decorate linings, bottoms, and tops.

Tapestry needle

Used to sew with yarn. Make sure the eye of the needle is wide enough to thread the yarn.

Wire and wire cutters

Used to make a flexible hemp handle.

basic crochet stitches

Chain Stitch (ch)

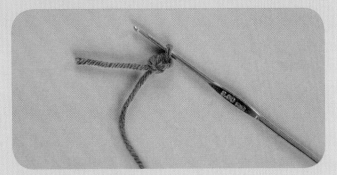

Insert hook in slip knot.

Yarn over and draw through loop on hook.

Continue this for as many chains as you need.

Single Crochet (sc)

Insert hook in next stitch or stitch indicated.

Yarn over, pull up a loop.

Yarn over and draw through both loops on hook.

Slip Stitch (sl st)

Insert hook in next stitch or stitch indicated.

Yarn over and draw through stitch and loop on hook.

Overlay Chain Stitch (overlay ch)

Insert hook into work (fabric) from front to back in stitch (place) indicated.

Yarn over, draw yarn through work (fabric)

and loop on hook.

Front Loop

Insert hook in top, front loop only (loop closest to you).

Complete the stitch.

Back Loop

Insert hook in top, back loop only (loop farthest from you).

Complete the stitch.

Double Crochet (dc)

Yarn over.

Insert hook in next stitch.

Yarn over.

Pull up a loop, yarn over, draw through 2 loops.

Yarn over, draw through 2 loops.

Half Double Crochet (hdc)

Yarn over, insert hook in next stitch or stitch indicated. Yarn over, pull up a loop.

Yarn over, and draw through all 3 loops on hook.

Treble Crochet (tr)

Yarn over twice.

Insert hook in next stitch or stitch indicated, yarn over. Pull up a loop,

(yarn over, draw though 2 loops) 3 times.

Half Treble Crochet (htr)

Yarn over twice. Insert hook in next stitch or stitch indicated, yarn over. Pull up a loop, yarn over and draw though 2 loops.

Yarn over, and draw through all 3 loops on hook.

special stitches

Long Single Crochet (lsc)

Insert hook in next stitch, 1 row below.

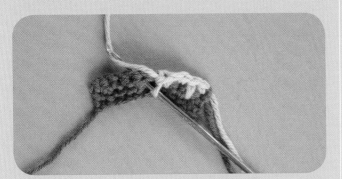

Yarn over.

Pull up a long loop, yarn over. Draw through both loops on hook to complete stitch.

Front Post Double Crochet Stitch (FP dc)

Yarn over, insert hook from front of next double crochet post to back, around post, and back to front.

Yarn over.

Pull up a loop. (Yarn over, draw through 2 loops on hook) twice to complete stitch.

Back Post Double Crochet Stitch (BP dc)

Yarn over, insert hook from behind next double crochet post to front, around post and to back.

Yarn over.

Pull up a loop. (Yarn over, draw through 2 loops on hook) twice to complete stitch.

Puff Stitch (Puff st)

Yarn over, skip next stitch, insert hook in next stitch.

Pull up a loop, yarn over.

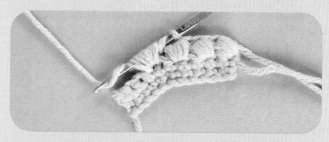

(Insert hook in same stitch and pull up a loop, yarn over) 4 times. Draw through all loops on hook.

Chain 1 to complete stitch.

Popcorn Stitch (Popcorn)

Yarn over, skip next stitch, insert hook in next stitch.

3 treble crochet in same stitch, remove hook from loop, insert hook from front to back in space to right of first treble crochet of 3-treble crochet group.

Pick up dropped loop.

Draw dropped loop through.
Chain 2 to complete stitch.

Loop Stitch (Loop st)

Loop stitch is created on backside while working.

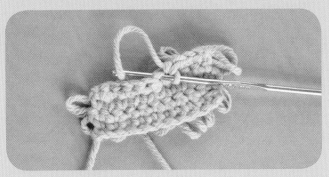

Wrap yarn around index finger, insert hook in next stitch, and grab yarn under index finger.

Pull up a loop, leaving formed loop over index finger. Drop loop to backside and pick up end of yarn.
Draw through both loops on hook to complete stitch.

Picot

Chain 3.

Insert hook in first stitch of this chain, yarn over. Draw through all loops on hook.

Skip next stitch (or as indicated), slip stitch in next stitch.

4 DC Filet

In 4 DC Filet, a mesh background is created by working double crochets with chain-2 spaces between each. Pictures are formed by filling in the spaces with double crochet.

To make an open mesh: chain 2, skip next 2 chains (or 2 double crochets), double crochet in next double crochet.

To make a solid mesh: dc in each of next 3 double crochet

or 2 double crochet in next chain-2 space (or in next 2 chains),

double crochet in next double crochet.

17

techniques

Fringes

Fold piece of yarn in half. Insert hook from front to back at bottom of stitch indicated.

Yarn over loose ends and pull them through loop on hook.

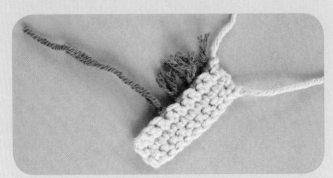

Pull on loose ends to draw them down snugly.

Trim ends to even them up.

Crocheting single crochet in holes

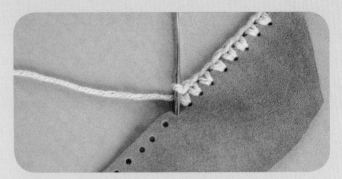

Insert hook in next hole.

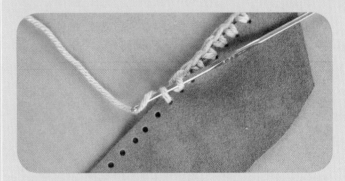

Yarn over, pull up a loop, yarn over and draw through both loops on hook.

Pompon

Copy template onto tracing paper. Cut out and transfer twice to cardboard; then cut out two cardboard discs. Lay cardboard discs on top of each other so that holes in centers are lined up. Thread needle with 2 strands of yarn, and wrap discs by drawing thread up through holes in center of discs, and around discs' outer edge. Wrap yarn snugly so that strands are close together, until the hole is filled.

Insert scissors between discs and cut yarn all around. Cut a 20"/50.8cm piece of yarn and tie tightly around middle of pompon, between discs. Leave tails for attaching pompon. Remove cardboard discs and trim yarn to make pompon even. Fluff up with a little steam.

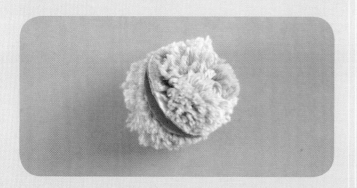

Pompon template

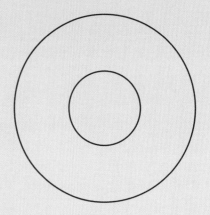

Flexible hemp handle

Fold wire in half. Make a 3"/7.6cm fold at one end of hemp rope. Place folded wire and folded end of hemp rope together so that folded end of hemp rope wraps top of wire.

With one hand, hold folded wire, hemp rope, and 3"/7.6cm tail of hemp yarn together (ball of hemp yarn is in other hand). Wrap hemp yarn tightly around folded wire, hemp rope, and hemp yarn tail, then continue wrapping folded wire and hemp rope all the way to end of wire. With hemp yarn and hemp rope, tie an overhand knot at the end, then cut hemp yarn leaving 3"/7.6cm tail.

Inserting chopstick handles

Position chopstick horizontally on top row of crocheted piece. Insert hook in next stitch in top row of crocheted piece.

Yarn over.

Pull up a loop.
Bringing hook over, and yarn from behind chopstick, yarn over and draw through both loops on hook.

Attaching snap top using crocheted circles for backing

With RS of circle facing, push top of snap (part with protruding center) prongs through,

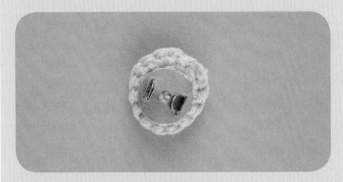

place washer, and push prongs down.

Position circle with snap top in appropriate place on WS of crocheted piece. Sew on with whip stitches that are not visible on RS of crocheted piece.

sewing stitches

Whip stitch

This is a simple over-and-over stitch that is used to connect two pieces.

Running stitch

In this stitch, the thread runs in a single direction without doubling back. Surface stitches should be of equal length. This stitch can be used to hold two pieces together.

terms and abbreviations

approx	approximately		**Popcorn**	Popcorn Stitch
beg	begin		**prev**	previous
BP dc	back post double crochet stitch		**Puff st**	Puff Stitch
ch(s)	chain stitch(es)		**rem**	remaining
cm	centimeter(s)		**rep**	repeat
cont	continue		**rnd(s)**	round(s)
dc	double crochet		**RS**	right side
FP dc	front post double crochet stitch		**sc**	single crochet
g	grams		**sk**	skip
hdc	half double crochet		**sl st**	slip stitch
htr	half triple crochet		**st(s)**	stitch(es)
Loop st	Loop Stitch		**tog**	together
lp(s)	loop(s)		**tr**	treble crochet
lsc	long single crochet		**WS**	wrong side
m	meter(s)		**yd**	yard
mm	millimeter			
overlay ch(s)	overlay chain stitch(es)			
oz	ounce			
PM	place marker			

fashionably striped "fabric" purse

This elegant purse is designed with the businesswoman in mind. Though the purse is completely crocheted, it has the look and feel of striped gabardine fabric.

EXPERIENCE LEVEL

■■■□ Intermediate

FINISHED MEASUREMENTS

9½"/24.1cm wide x 11"27.9cm high x 1"/2.5cm deep

MATERIALS AND TOOLS

Yarn A **MEDIUM 4**: 414yd/381m of Medium weight yarn, wool/silk, in purple with white specs

Yarn B **MEDIUM 4**: 197yd/180m of Worsted weight yarn, acrylic/wool, in light pink

Yarn C **MEDIUM 4**: 197yd/180m of Worsted weight yarn, acrylic/wool, in deep pinkish purple

Straight pins

Sewing needle and thread matching Yarn C

Two purple faux leather purse handles, 13"/33cm wide

GAUGE

With Yarn A, 12 sts and 10 rows = 2"/5cm in sc

SPECIAL STITCHES

Puff Stitch (Puff st) (page 15)

instructions

FRONT AND BACK (MAKE 2)

Note: This purse looks like it is made from vertically striped fabric. The "fabric" is actually crocheted horizontally, so bottom of front and back become side of front and back when finished.

With Yarn A, ch 60.

Row 1: Ch 1, sc into 2nd ch from hook and in each of next rem chs—60 sc.

Row 2: Join Yarn B, ch 1, sc in 1st sc from hook and in each of next 2 sc, Puff st in next sc; *sc in each of next 3 sc, Puff st in next sc. Rep from * 13 times. Sc in each of next rem 4 sc—14 Puff sts. Cut yarn.

Row 3: With Yarn A, ch 1, sc in 1st sc from hook and in each of next 3 sc; *sc in Puff st, sc in each of next 3 sc. Rep from * 14 times.

Row 4: Ch 1, sc into 1st sc from hook and in each of next rem sc—60 sc.

Row 5: Ch 4, sk 1st sc from hook, dc in next sc; *ch 1, sk next sc, dc in next sc. Rep from * 29 times—30 dc.

Row 6: Ch 1, sc in 1st ch-1 space of prev row; *sc in next dc, sc in next ch-1 space. Rep from * 29 times. End with sc in 3rd ch of ch-4 of prev row—60 sc.

Row 7: Ch 1, sc into 1st sc from hook and in each of next rem sc—60 sc.

Row 8: Join Yarn C, ch 1, sc in 1st sc from hook and in each of next 2 sc, Puff st in next sc; *sc in each of next 3 sc, Puff st in next sc. Rep from * 13 times. Sc in each of next rem 4 sc—14 Puff sts. Cut yarn.

Rows 9–13: Rep rows 3–7.

Row 14: Rep row 2.

Rows 15–19: Rep rows 3–7.

Row 20: Rep row 8.

Rows 21–22: Rep rows 3–4.

Row 23: Ch 5, sk 1st sc from hook, tr in next sc; *ch 1, sk next sc, tr in next sc. Rep from * 29 times—30 tr.

Row 24: Ch 1, sc in 1st ch-1 space of prev row; *sc in next tr, sc in next ch-1 space. Rep from * 29 times. End with sc in 4th ch of ch-5 of prev row—60 sc.

Row 25: Rep row 7.

Row 26: Rep row 8.

Rows 27–31: Rep rows 3–7.

Row 32: Rep row 2.

Rows 33–37: Rep rows 3–7.

Row 38: Rep row 8.

Rows 39–43: Rep rows 3–7.

Row 44: Rep row 2.

Row 45: Rep row 3. Don't cut Yarn A. Cont with 3 sc in the corner. Work along bottom and sc in each 'sc' row, 2 sc in dc spaces and 3 sc in tr space; 3 sc in next corner; cont along one side, from bottom to top, and sc in each ch of foundation chs. Count sts when working—177 sc. Fasten off.

SIDES AND BOTTOM

With Yarn A, ch 177.

Row 1: Ch 1, sc into 2nd ch from hook and in each of next rem chs—177 sc.

Rows 2–4: Ch 1, sc into 1st sc from hook and in each of next rem sc—177 sc. Fasten off.

HANDLE HOLDER (MAKE 4)

With Yarn C, ch 4.

Row 1: Ch 1, sc into 2nd ch from hook and in each of next rem chs—4 sc.

Rows 2–4: Ch 1, sc into 1st sc from hook and in each of next rem sc—4 sc. Fasten off.

ATTACHING HANDLE HOLDER AND HANDLE (REP 4 TIMES)

With RS of front (back) facing and bottom close to you, place top of handle holder on 2nd light pink strip from right (left) side and 2"/5cm from top of front (back), and pin. Sew on handle holder top with a few invisible sts. Draw handle loop onto handle holder, then sew on handle holder bottom.

STRAP HOLDER

With Yarn C, ch 4.

Row 1: Ch 1, sc into 2nd ch from hook and in each of next rem chs—4 sc.

Rows 2–11: Ch 1, sc into 1st sc from hook and in each of next rem sc—4 sc. Fasten off.

ATTACHING STRAP HOLDER

With RS of front facing and bottom close to you, position strap holder horizontally across front middle, 3"/7.6cm from top. Sew on left and right edge of strap holder with a few sts that are not visible from RS.

ATTACHING FRONT AND BACK TO SIDES AND BOTTOM

With RS of front and WS of side and bottom facing, bottom to your left, and Yarn C, insert hook in front lp of 1st sc in last row of front and in 1st ch of foundation chs of sides and bottom, ch 1, sc in same pair of sts; sc in each of next rem pairs along front sides and bottom. Fasten off.

With RS of back and WS of side and bottom facing, bottom to your left, and Yarn C, insert hook in front lp of 1st sc in last row of back and in 1st sc in last row of sides and bottom, ch 1, sc in same pair of sts; sc in each of next rem pairs along back sides and bottom. Fasten off.

CROCHETED TOP EDGE

With RS of purse facing, bottom close to you, and Yarn A, insert hook in one corner at top edge of purse, ch 1, and work round this edge and sc in each 'sc' row, 2 sc in dc spaces and 3 sc in tr space. Join with sl st in 1st sc. Fasten off.

FASTENING STRAP

With RS of back facing and bottom close to you, mark center 9 sts on edge of back. Join Yarn A at rightmost st.
Row 1: Ch 1, sc in same st, sc in each of next 8 sc on edge of back—9 sc.
Rows 2–50: Ch 1, sc in 1st sc from hook and in each of next 8 sc—9 sc.
Row 51: Ch 1, sk 1st sc from hook, sc in each of next 6 sc, sk next sc, sc in last sc—7 sc.
Row 52: Ch 1, sk 1st sc from hook, sc in each of next 4 sc, sk next sc, sc in last sc—5 sc. Fasten off.

this project was knit with

(A) 3 balls of Moda dea Silk'n Wool Blend, 85% wool/15% silk, medium weight yarn, 2.8oz/80g = approx 138yd/127m, color #4278

(B) 1 ball of Lion Wool-Ease, 80% acrylic/20%wool, worsted weight yarn, 3oz/85g = approx 197yd/180m per ball, color #620-104

(C) 1 ball of Lion Wool-Ease, 80% acrylic/20%wool, worsted weight yarn, 3oz/85g = approx 197yd/180m per ball, color #620-139

elegant pompon purse

This chic black and white purse is made from super-soft yarn. Decorated with playful handmade pompons, it's both elegant and fun.

EXPERIENCE LEVEL

◼◼◻◻ Easy

FINISHED MEASUREMENTS

13"/33cm wide x 9½"/24.1cm high

MATERIALS AND TOOLS

Yarn A **6 SUPER BULKY**: 84yd/80m of Super bulky yarn, wool/nylon, in white

Yarn B **6 SUPER BULKY**: 42yd/40m of Super bulky yarn, wool/nylon, in deep gray

Yarn C **6 SUPER BULKY**: 106yd/97m of Super bulky yarn, acrylic/wool, in cream with black

Yarn D **6 SUPER BULKY**: 106yd/97m of Super bulky yarn, acrylic/wool, in dark gray

Size K/10 ½ (6.5mm) crochet hook OR SIZE TO OBTAIN GAUGE

Tapestry needle

Place marker

For pompons:

Tracing paper

Pencil

Scissors

Piece of cardboard

GAUGE

With Yarn C, 5 sts and 5 rows = 2"/5cm in sc

SPECIAL STITCHES

Long Single Crochet (lsc) (page 14)

TECHNIQUES

Pompon (page 19)

instructions

OVAL BOTTOM

With Yarn C, ch 21.

Rnd 1: 6 sc in the 2nd ch from hook, sc in each of next 18 chs, 6 sc in last ch. Don't turn. Work along bottom side of foundation chs, sc in unused lps of next 18 chs, join with sl st in 1st sc—48 sc. Don't cut yarn.

Rnd 2: Join Yarn D, ch 1, 2 sc in same sc as joining, 2 sc in each of next 5 sc, sc in each of next 18 sc, 2 sc in each of next 6 sc, sc in each of next 18 sc, join with sl st in 1st sc—60 sc. Don't cut yarn.

Rnd 3: With Yarn C, ch 1, sc in same sc as joining, 2 sc in next sc, *sc in next sc, 2 sc in next sc. Rep from * 5 times. Sc in each of next 18 sc, **sc in next sc, 2 sc in next sc. Rep from ** 6 times. Sc in each of next 18 sc, join with sl st in 1st sc—72 sc. Don't cut yarn.

Rnd 4: With Yarn D, ch 1, inserting hook in back lp only, sc in same sc as joining and in each rem sc, join with sl st in back lp of 1st sc. Don't cut yarn.

Rnd 5: With Yarn C, ch 1, sc in same sc as joining, lsc in next st 1 rnd below, *sk st behind lsc, sc in next sc, lsc in next st 1 rnd below. Rep from * all around. Join with sl st in 1st sc. Cut yarn.

Rnd 6: With Yarn D, ch 1, lsc in same st as joining 1 rnd below, sk st behind lsc, sc in next lsc, *lsc in next st 1 rnd below, sk st behind lsc, sc in next lsc. Rep from * all around. Join with sl st in 1st lsc. Cut yarn.

BODY

Rnd 1: With Yarn A, ch 1, inserting hook in back lp only, sc in same lsc as joining and in each st around, join with sl st in back lp of 1st sc—72 sc.

Rnds 2–8: Ch 1, sc in same sc as joining and in each rem sc, join with sl st in 1st sc.

Rnd 9: Ch 1, 2 sc in same sc as joining, sc in each of next 16 sc, 2 sc in next sc, sc in each of next 18 sc, 2 sc in next sc, sc in each of next 16 sc, 2 sc in next sc, sc in each of next 18 sc, join with sl st in 1st sc—76 sc.

Rnds 10–14: Ch 1, sc in same sc as joining and in each rem sc, join with sl st in 1st sc. Cut yarn.

Rnd 15: Join Yarn B, ch 1, sc in same sc as joining, lsc in next st 1 rnd below, *sk st behind lsc, sc in next sc, lsc in next st 1 rnd below. Rep from * all around. Join with sl st in 1st sc. Cut yarn.

Rnd 16: Join Yarn D, ch 1, sc in same sc as joining and in each st all around, join with sl st in 1st sc.

Rnd 17: Ch 1, sc in same sc as joining and in each rem sc, join with sl st in 1st sc. Do not cut.

Rnd 18: Join C, ch 1, sc in same sc as joining, lsc in next st 1 rnd below, *sk st behind lsc, sc in next sc, lsc in next st 1 rnd below. Rep from * all around. Join with sl st in 1st sc. Cut yarn.

Rnd 19: With Yarn D, ch 1, lsc in same st as joining 1 rnd below, sk st behind lsc, sc in next lsc, *lsc in next st 1 rnd below, sk st behind lsc, sc in next lsc. Rep from * all around. Join with sl st in 1st lsc.

Rnd 20: Ch 1, sc in same lsc as joining and in each st all around, join with sl st in 1st lsc. Cut yarn.

Note for Rnd 21: Count sts when working and PM in 22nd and 60th sc.

Rnd 21: Join Yarn B, ch 1, sc in same sc as joining and in each rem sc, join with sl st in 1st sc. Fasten off.

HANDLES (MAKE 2)

Row 1: With RS of front (back) facing and Yarn D, insert hook into 22nd (60th) sc from joining st of last rnd, ch 1, sc in same sc and in each of next 14 sc—15 sc.

Row 2: Ch 1, sc in 1st sc from hook, *lsc in next st 1 row below, sk st behind lsc, sc in next sc. Rep from * across.

Row 3: Ch 1, lsc in 1st sc from hook, *sk st behind lsc, sc in next lsc, lsc in next st 1 row below. Rep from * across.

Row 4: Ch 1, sc in 1st lsc from hook, *lsc in next st 1 row below, sk st behind lsc, sc in next lsc. Rep from * across.

Row 5 (gap): Ch 1, sk 1st sc from hook, sc in next lsc, lsc in next st 1 row below, sk st behind lsc, sc in next lsc, ch 7, join with sc in 12th st of prev row, lsc in next st 1 row below, sk st behind lsc and next st, sc in last st—13 sts.

Row 6: Ch 1, sk 1st sc from hook, sc in next lsc, lsc in next st 1 row below, sk st behind lsc, work 7 sc under ch-7 sts of prev row (into gap), lsc in joining st 1 row below, sk st behind lsc and next st, sc in last st—11 sts.

Row 7: Ch 1, sk 1st sc from hook, sc in next lsc, *lsc into gap, sk st behind lsc, sc in next sc. Rep from * 3 times. Lsc into gap, sk st behind lsc and next st, sc in last st—9 sts.

Row 8: Ch 1, sk 1st sc from hook, sc in next lsc, *lsc in next st 1 row below, sk st behind lsc, sc in next lsc. Rep from * twice. Lsc in next st 1 row below, sk st behind lsc and next st, sc in last st—7 sts.

CROCHETED TOP EDGE AND HANDLES

With Yarn B, insert hook into 1st sc of last rnd of body, ch 1, sc in same sc and in each sc of this rnd to 1st handle, sc in each st of last row of handle, cont with sc in each sc of last rnd of the body to 2nd handle, sc in each st of last row of handle, sc in rem sc of body, join with sl st in 1st sc. Fasten off.

POMPON (MAKE 2)

Make one pompon with 2 strands of D and another pompon with 1 strand each of C and D.

RIBBON

With Yarn D, ch 50. Cut yarn, tie ends, and hide tails.

Thread tail from pompon onto tapestry needle and sew one pompon onto either end of ribbon.

Decide where to position pompons and place ribbon so that one pompon hangs a bit lower than the other. Sew ribbon onto bag with a few simple stitches and tie into a bow.

this project was crocheted with

(A) 4 balls of Lion Sasha, 96% wool/4% nylon, super bulky weight, approx 1.75oz/50g = approx 21yd/20m per ball, color 690-100

(B) 2 balls of Lion Sasha, 96% wool/4% nylon, super bulky weight, approx 1.75oz/50g = approx 21yd/20m per ball, color 690-153

(C) 1 ball of Lion Wool-Ease Thick & Quick, 80% acrylic/20% wool, super bulky weight, approx 6oz/170g = approx 106yd/97m per ball, color 640-402

(D) 1 ball of Lion Wool-Ease Thick & Quick, 80% acrylic/20% wool, super bulky weight, approx 6oz/170g = approx 106yd/97m per ball, color 640-149

stylish grocery tote

This entire bag, including the handles, is crocheted in a single piece and secured at the top with an elegant crocheted "belt". Attach the Spiral Change Purse (page 37) for storing small change and keys.

EXPERIENCE LEVEL

■■□□ Easy

FINISHED MEASUREMENTS

- 10½"/27cm wide x 12"/30.5cm high

MATERIALS AND TOOLS

- Yarn A **(5 BULKY)**: 252yd/232m of Chunky weight yarn, bamboo/acrylic/polyester, in off-white
- Yarn B **(4 MEDIUM)**: 207yd/188m of Worsted weight yarn, cotton/acrylic, in dark olive green
- Yarn C **(4 MEDIUM)**: 207yd/188m of Worsted weight yarn, cotton/acrylic, in dark yellow
- Size E/4 (3.5mm) crochet hook OR SIZE TO OBTAIN GAUGE

GAUGE

- With Yarn A, 5 sts and 5 rows = 3"/7.6cm in dc, ch 2 patt

SPECIAL STITCHES

- Picot: Ch 3, sl st in 1st ch of ch-3 (page 17)

instructions

SPIRAL BODY WITH HANDLES

Note: The rounds in this project are actually spirals that are worked around without interruption.

With Yarn A, ch 6, join with sl st in 1st ch to form a ring.

Rnd 1: Ch 1, 9 sc in ring.

Rnd 2: 2 sc in each sc of prev rnd—18 sc.

Rnd 3: Sc in each sc of prev rnd—18 sc.

Rnds 4–6: *Ch 1, sc in next sc of prev rnd. Rep from * 18 times.

Rnd 7: *Ch 2, sc in next ch-1 space of prev rnd. Rep from * 18 times.

Rnd 8: *Ch 2, sc in next ch-2 space of prev rnd, ch 2, (sc, ch 2, sc) in next ch-2 space. Rep from * 9 times—27 sc and 27 ch-2 spaces.

Rnds 9–10: *Ch 2, sc in next ch-2 space of prev rnd. Rep from * 27 times.

Rnd 11: *Ch 2, sc in next ch-2 space of prev rnd, ch 2, sc in next ch-2 space, ch 2, (sc, ch 2, sc) in next ch-2 space. Rep from * 9 times—36 sc and 36 ch-2 spaces.

Rnds 12–17: *Ch 2, sc in next ch-2 space of prev rnd. Rep from * 36 times.

Rnd 18: *Ch 2, hdc in next ch-2 space of prev rnd. Rep from * 36 times—36 hdc and 36 ch-2 spaces.

Rnds 19–30: *Ch 2, dc in next ch-2 space of prev rnd. Rep from * 36 times—36 dc and 36 ch-2 spaces.

Rnd 31: *Ch 2, dc in next ch-2 space of prev rnd. Rep from * 36 times. Join with sl st in 1st dc—36 dc and 36 ch-2 spaces.

Rnd 32: Ch 1, 2 sc in 1st ch-2 space of prev rnd, sk next dc; *2 sc in next ch-2 space, sk next dc. Rep from * 35 times. Join with a sl st in 1st sc—72 sc.

Rnd 33: Ch 1, sc in joining st and in each of next 71 sc— 72 sc. Don't cut yarn.

HANDLES

Note: Continue working on body for handles.

Rnd 1: Ch 64 for 1st handle, join with sl st in 20th sc from joining st of prev rnd; sc in each of next 16 sc. For 2nd handle, sl st in next sc, ch 64, join with sl st in 20th sc from 1st sl st of this handle; sc in each of next 16 sc. Join with sl st in 1st ch of ch-64.

Rnd 2: Ch 1, sc in joining st and in each of next 63 chs of 1st handle; sk next sl st, sc in each of next 16 sc; sc in each of next 64 chs of 2nd handle; sk next sl st, sc in each of next 16 sc. Join with sl st in 1st sc. Cut yarn.

Rnd 3: Join Yarn B, ch 3, sl st in 1st ch of ch-3, sk joining st, sl st in next sc of 1st handle; *picot, sk next sc, sl st in next sc. Rep from * 31 times along 1st handle; 8 times around tote body; 32 times along 2nd handle; 8 times around tote body. Join with sl st in 1st ch from beg of rnd. Fasten off.

(Rep twice)

With RS facing, bottom close to you, and Yarn B, insert hook in rightmost sc of last rnd of body under one handle, ch 1, sc in same sc and in each of next 15 sc along tote body to leftmost sc under handle; sc in unused lps of next 64 chs of foundation row of handle. Join with sl st in 1st sc. Fasten off.

BELT

With Yarn A, ch 160.

Row 1: Ch 1, sc in 2nd ch from hook and in each of next 159 chs.

Rnd 2: Join Yarn B, picot, sk 1st sc; *sl st in next sc, picot, sk next sc. Rep from * 79 times. Cont working along bottom in unused lps of foundation chs, picot; *sl st in unused lp of 1st ch, picot, sk next ch. Rep from * 79 times. Join with sl st in 1st ch. Fasten off.

With RS facing and bottom close to you, insert belt into 31st round of body in 2nd space to right of front middle, in space between 2 dc sts, and draw out in next space. Insert in 7th space to the right, and draw out in next space. Insert in 8th space to the right (back middle) and draw out in next space. Insert in 8th space to the right, and draw out in next space. Insert in 7th space to the right and draw out in next space. You should now be in 2nd space to the left of front middle.

this project was crocheted with

(A) 4 balls of Bernat Bamboo, 86% bamboo/12% acrylic/2% polyester, chunky weight, 2.1oz/60g = approx 63yd/58m per ball, color #92008

(B) 1 ball of Lion Cotton-Ease, 50% cotton/50% acrylic, worsted weight, 3.5oz/100g = approx 207yd/188m per ball, color #830-132

(C) 1 ball of Lion Cotton-Ease, 50% cotton/50% acrylic, worsted weight, 3.5oz/100g = approx 207yd/188m per ball, color #830-186

spiral change purse

This round purse is a perfect accompaniment to the Stylish Grocery Tote (page 33). It can be attached to the tote belt (see photo page 35) or left loose inside the tote. Its Velcro closure keeps the purse securely closed; the flowery loop adds a decorative touch.

EXPERIENCE LEVEL

■■ □ □ Easy

FINISHED MEASUREMENTS

3½"/8.9cm in diameter

MATERIALS AND TOOLS

Yarn A **[5] BULKY**: 63yd/58m of Chunky weight yarn, bamboo/acrylic/polyester, in off-white

Yarn B **[4] MEDIUM**: 207yd/188m of Worsted weight yarn, cotton/acrylic, in dark olive green

Yarn C **[4] MEDIUM**: 207yd/188m of Worsted weight yarn, cotton/acrylic, in dark yellow

Size E/4 (3.5mm) crochet hook OR SIZE TO OBTAIN GAUGE

One piece of Velcro, 2"/5cm long

Sewing needle and thread

One orange shank button, ¼"/0.6cm diameter

GAUGE

With Yarn A, 5 sts and 4 rows = 1"/2.5cm in sc

SPECIAL STITCHES

Picot: Ch 3, sl st in 1st ch of ch-3 (page 17)

instructions

DISC (MAKE 2)

With Yarn A, ch 6, join with sl st in 1st ch to form a ring.

Rnd 1: Ch 1, 9 sc in ring.

Rnd 2: Inserting hook in back lp only, 2 sc in each sc of prev rnd—18 sc.

Rnd 3: Inserting hook in back lp only, 2 sc in 1st sc of prev rnd, sc in next sc; *2 sc in back lp of next sc, sc in next sc. Rep from * 8 times—27 sc.

Rnd 4: Inserting hook in back lp only, 2 sc in 1st sc of prev rnd, sc in next 2 sc; *2 sc in back lp of next sc, sc in next 2 sc. Rep from * 8 times—36 sc.

Rnd 5: Inserting hook in back lp only, 2 sc in 1st sc of prev rnd, sc in next 3 sc; *2 sc in back lp of next sc, sc in next 3 sc. Rep from * 8 times—45 sc.

Rnd 6: Inserting hook in back lp only, 2 sc in 1st sc of prev rnd, sc in next 4 sc; *2 sc in back lp of next sc, sc in next 4 sc. Rep from * 8 times—54 sc.

Rnd 7: Inserting hook in back lp only, 2 sc in 1st sc of prev rnd, sc in next 5 sc; *2 sc in back lp of next sc, sc in next 5 sc. Rep from * 8 times. Join with sl st in 1st sc—63 sc. Cut yarn.

ATTACHING VELCRO

With WS of front (back) facing, position left corner of front (back) of Velcro piece ¼"/0.6cm (1¾"/4.5cm) from last round joining st, and ¼"/0.6cm from edge. Sew on with a few hidden sts.

ATTACHING DISCS

Note: Connect front and back discs, leaving an opening at the top where the Velcro is attached.

Place 2 discs with WS tog. With Yarn C, insert hook in front lp of last rnd joining st in upper disc, and in back lp of same st in lower disc. *Picot, sk next sc in both discs, sl st in front lp of next sc in upper disc and in back lp of next sc in lower disc. Rep from * 23 times. Cont working around each disc separately to form opening.

CROCHETED OPENING

For upper disc only, picot; *sk next sc at top disc, sl st in front lp of next sc in front shape, picot. Rep from * 7 times. Join with sl st in front lp of last rnd joining st of top disc and in back lp of same st in bottom disc. Cut yarn.

For lower disc only, with Yarn C, insert hook in back lp of sc of last picot at bottom disc, *picot, sk next sc of bottom disc, sl st in back lp of next sc of bottom disc, picot. Rep from * 7 times. Join with sl st in back lp of last rnd joining st of bottom disc. Fasten off.

DECORATIVE CLOSURE

Flowery loop

With Yarn C, ch 12, join with sl st in 1st ch to form a ring.

Rnd 1: *Picot, sc in ring. Rep from * 5 times. Join with sl st in 1st ch of ch-3. Cut yarn and tie ends. Don't hide tails.

Stem

With RS of back disc facing and Yarn B, insert hook in last rnd st at back middle of opening, ch 10. Cut yarn and tie ends. Don't hide tails.

With RS of front disc facing, insert hook in last rnd st at back middle of opening and draw stem out. Attach flowery loop to stem by sewing on one of the petals.

Sew on button at center front of top disc.

Note: To attach change purse to grocery bag belt, sew one end of belt to middle of change purse back with a few hidden sts. Draw belt along back of change purse and sew together again at other end of change purse.

this project was crocheted with

(A) 1 ball of Bernat Bamboo, 86% bamboo/12% acrylic/2% polyester, chunky weight, 2.1oz/60g = approx 63yd/58m per ball, color #92008

(B) 1 ball of Lion Cotton-Ease, 50% cotton/50% acrylic, worsted weight, 3.5oz/100g = approx 207yd/188m per ball, color #830-132

(C) 1 ball of Lion Cotton-Ease, 50% cotton/50% acrylic, worstd weight, 3.5oz/100g = approx 207yd/188m per ball, color #830-186

classic campus backpack

Inspired by book bags of the 1920s and 1930s, this backpack has two external pockets and one internal pocket. Sturdy and stylish, it features thick hemp straps and attractive wooden buttons.

EXPERIENCE LEVEL

Intermediate

FINISHED MEASUREMENTS

- 12½"/31.8cm wide x 11"/27.9cm high x 3½"/8.9cm deep

MATERIALS AND TOOLS

- Yarn A **SUPER BULKY 6** : 400yd/360m of Super bulky yarn, acrylic/rayon, in khaki

- Yarn B **SUPER BULKY 6** : 100yd/90m of Super bulky yarn, acrylic/rayon, in white

- Yarn C **SUPER BULKY 6** : 106yd/97m of Super bulky yarn, acrylic/wool, in cream

- Yarn D **SUPER BULKY 6** : 212yd/194m of Super bulky yarn, acrylic/wool, in brown

- Size H/8 (5mm) crochet hook OR SIZE TO OBTAIN GAUGE

- Eight 2-hole wooden buttons, ¾"/1.9cm diameter

- Place marker

- Two buckles with leather belt loop, 2"/5cm wide x 1½"/3.8cm long

- Four hemp straps: Two: 2¼"/5.5cm wide x 6"/15.2cm long; and two: 2¼"/5.5cm wide x 21"/53.3cm long

- Straight pins

- Tapestry needle

GAUGE

- With Yarn A, 6 sts and 6 rows = 2"/5cm in sc

SEWING STITCHES

- Running Stitch (page 21)

instructions

FRONT AND BACK (MAKE 2)

Note: The pieces of this bag are crocheted separately and then attached. Marking the connection points (a through h) as you go makes it easier to explain where to attach the pieces later.

For front, PM: 3rd row 4th st (a); 3rd row 17th st (b); 3rd row 20th st (c); 3rd row 33rd st (d); 18th row 4th st (e); 18th row 17th st (f); 18th row 20th st (g); 18th row 33rd st (h)

With Yarn A, ch 36.

Row 1: Ch 1, sc into 2nd ch from hook and in each of next rem chs—36 sc.

Rows 2–32: Ch 1, sc in 1st sc from hook and in each of next rem sc—36 sc. Cut yarn.

FLAP

Row 1: With WS of back facing and Yarn A, insert hook in back lp of rightmost sc at last row of back, ch 1, sc in 1st st and in each rem sc—36 sc.

Rows 2–16: Ch 1, sc in 1st sc from hook and in each of next rem sc—36 sc.

Row 17: Ch 1, sc in 1st sc from hook and in each of next 9 sc, ch 3 for 1st buttonhole, sk next 3 sc, sc in each of next 10 sc, ch 3 for 2nd buttonhole, sk next 3 sc, sc in each of next 10 sc.

Row 18: Ch 1, sc in 1st sc from hook and in each of next 9 sc, 3 sc in ch-3 space, sc in each of next 10 sc, 3 sc in ch-3 space, sc in each of next 10 sc.

Row 19: Ch 1, sk 1st sc from hook, sc in each of next 33 sc, sk next sc, sc in next sc—34 sc.

Row 20: Ch 1, sk 1st sc from hook, sc in each of next 31 sc, sk next sc, sc in next sc—32 sc. Fasten off.

FRONT POCKETS

Left pocket foundation

With RS of front facing, bottom to your left, and Yarn C, insert hook in 18th row 4th st (e). Work 15 overlay chs along left side of front, from top to bottom, inserting hook in each next row 4th st—you will now be at (a). With front bottom close to you, work another 13 overlay chs along front bottom, inserting hook in each next st of 3rd row—you will now be at (b). With front bottom to your right, work another 15 overlay chs along sides of front, from bottom to top, inserting hook in each next row 17th st—you will now be at (f). Cut yarn.

Right pocket foundation

With RS of front facing, bottom to your left and Yarn C, insert hook in 18th row 20th st (g). Work 15 overlay chs along sides of front, from top to bottom, inserting hook in each next row 20th st—you will now be at (c). With front bottom close to you, work another 13 overlay chs along front bottom, inserting hook in each next st of 3rd row—you will now be at (d). With front bottom at your right, work another 15 overlay chs along right side of front, from bottom to top, inserting hook in each next row 33rd st—you will now be at (h). Cut yarn.

Pocket sides and bottom (make 2)

Row 1: With Yarn C, insert hook in 1st overlay ch of left (right) pocket foundation, ch 1, sc in same st and in each of next rem overlay chs across pocket foundation—43 sc.

Row 2: Ch 1, sc in 1st sc from hook and in each of next rem sc—43 sc. Fasten off. You now have 43 sc; 15 sc on each side, and 13 sc at the bottom.

Pocket front (make 2)

Row 1: With RS of front facing, bottom close to you and Yarn A, insert hook in back lp of rightmost bottom sc at last row of left (right) pocket bottom, ch 1, sc in same lp and in each back lp of next 12 sc along pocket bottom.

Rows 2–14: Ch 1, sc in 1st sc from hook and in each of next rem sc—13 sc. Fasten off.

Attaching pocket front (make 2)

With RS of front facing, bottom to your left and Yarn D, insert hook in 1st st at right edge of last row of pocket front and in back lp of 1st sc at last row of pocket's right side. Ch 1, sc in same pair of sts, sc in each of next 13 pairs along pocket's right side, from bottom to top, 3 sc in back lp of next sc at last row of pocket's right side, sc in unused lps of next13 sc along pocket bottom, 3 sc in back lp of next sc in last row of pocket's left side, sc in 1st st at left edge in 1st row of pocket front and in back lp of next sc in last row of pocket's left side, sc in each of next 13 pairs along pocket's left side from bottom to top. Fasten off.

Pocket flap (make 2)

With RS of front facing, bottom close to you and Yarn A, insert hook in (e) for left pocket (in (g) for right pocket). Work 13 overlay chs along front bottom, inserting hook in each next st of 18th row. Cut yarn.

Row 1: With RS of front facing, bottom close to you, and Yarn A, insert hook in 1st overlay ch of pocket flap foundation, ch 1, sc in same st and in each of next rem overlay chs along pocket flap foundation—13 sc.

Rows 2–4: Ch 1, sc in 1st sc from hook and in each of next rem sc—13 sc.

Row 5: Ch 1, sc in 1st sc from hook and in each of next 4 sc, ch 2 for buttonhole, sk next 2 sc, sc in each of next 6 sc.

Row 6: Ch 1, sc in 1st sc from hook and in each of next 5 sc, 2 sc in ch-2 space, sc in each of next 5 sc.

Row 7: Ch 1, sk 1st sc from hook, sc in each of next 10 sc, sk next sc, sc in next sc—11sc.

Row 8: Ch 1, sk 1st sc from hook, sc in each of next 8 sc, sk next sc, sc in next sc—9 sc. Cut yarn.

With RS of front facing, bottom to your left, and Yarn D, insert hook in 1st st at right edge of 1st row of pocket flap, ch 1, sc in same st and in each of next sts along right edge of pocket flap, 3 sc in corner st, sc in each of next 9 sc of last row of pocket flap, 3 sc in corner st, sc in each of next 1st sts along left edge of pocket flap. Fasten off.

INTERIOR POCKET

Pocket foundation

With WS of back facing, bottom to your left, and Yarn C, insert hook in 26th row 6th st. Work 20 overlay chs along left side of back, from top to bottom, inserting hook in each next row 6th st—you will now be at 6th row 6th st. With back bottom close to you, work another 25 overlay chs along back bottom, inserting hook in each next st of 6th row—you will now be at 6th row 31st st. With back bottom to your right, work another 20 overlay chs along sides of back, from bottom to top, inserting hook in each next row 31st st—you will now be at 26th row 31st st. Cut yarn. You now have 65 sc; 20 sc for each side, and 25 sc for the bottom.

Pocket sides and bottom

Row 1: With Yarn C, insert hook in 1st overlay ch of pocket foundation, ch 1, sc in same st and in each of next rem overlay chs across pocket foundation—65 sc. Fasten off.

Pocket front

Row 1: With WS of back facing, bottom close to you, and Yarn B, insert hook in back lp of rightmost bottom sc at last row of pocket bottom (21st sc), ch 1, sc in same lp and in each back lp of next 24 sc along pocket bottom.

Rows 2–19: Ch 1, sc in 1st sc from hook and in each of next rem sc—25 sc. Fasten off.

Attaching pocket front

With WS of back facing, bottom to your left, and Yarn D, insert hook in 1st st at right edge in last row of pocket front and back lp of 1st sc in last row of pocket right side. Ch 1, sc in same pair of sts, sc in each of next 18 pairs along pocket right side, from top to bottom, 3 sc in back lp of next sc in last row of pocket right side, sc in unused lps of next 25 sc along pocket bottom, 3 sc in back lp of next sc in last row of pocket's left side, sc in 1st st at left edge in 1st row of pocket front and in back lp of next sc in last row of pocket's left side, sc in each of next 18 pairs along pocket's left side, from bottom to top. Fasten off. Note: You now have 100 rows; 32 rows for each side, and 36 rows for the bottom.

BACKPACK SIDES AND BOTTOM

With Yarn D, ch 10.

Row 1: Ch 1, sc into 2nd ch from hook and in each of next rem chs—10 sc.

Rows 2–100: Ch 1, sc in 1st sc from hook and in each of next rem sc—10 sc. Cut yarn.

ATTACHING BACK HEMP STRAP (REP TWICE)

Make a 1"/2.5cm fold at each edge of larger hemp strap and pin. Consider side of strap with folded area as back of strap. With RS of backpack back facing and bottom close to you, position one hemp strap end, with back facing and other end upwards, 2"/5cm below backpack flap and 3"/7.6cm from left (right) edge, and pin.

With Yarn D, sew folded part of strap in place with 3 rows of running stitch. Sew decorative X-shape over top 2 rows.

With front side of strap facing, sew buckle ½"/1.3cm from loose hemp end.

ATTACHING DECORATIVE HEMP STRAP (REP TWICE)

With RS of backpack side facing, position shorter hemp strap lengthwise 7"/18cm from each end of backpack side. Using Yarn D, secure strap by sewing around parameter with running stitch.

ATTACHING BACKPACK SIDES AND BOTTOM TO BACKPACK FRONT AND BACK

With RS of front and WS of side facing, bottom to your left, and Yarn D, insert hook in 1st st at right edge of front top and 1st st at one edge of side top. Ch 1, sc in same pair of sts, sc in each of next 30 pairs along front right edge, from top to bottom, 3 sc in next pair of sts (corner), sc in each of next 36 pairs of foundation chs of front and 1st sts at edge of side along front bottom, 3 sc in next pair of sts (corner), sc in each of next 36 pairs of 1st sts at left edge of front and in 1st sts at edge of side along front left edge from bottom to top. Fasten off.

With RS of back and WS of side facing, bottom to your left, and Yarn D, insert hook in 1st st at right edge of back top (under flap) and 1st st at other edge of side top. Ch 1, sc in same pair of sts, sc in each of next 30 pairs along back right edge, from top to bottom, 3 sc in next pair of sts (corner), sc in each of next 36 pairs of foundation chs of back and 1st sts at edge of side along back bottom, 3 sc in next pair of sts (corner), sc in each of next 36 pairs of 1st sts at left edge of back and in 1st sts at edge of side along back left edge from bottom to top. Cont with sc in each of next 1st sts at right edge of flap along right edge of flap from bottom to top, 3 sc in corner st, sc in each of next 32 sc at last row of flap, 3 sc in corner st, sc in each of next 1st sts along left edge of pocket flap, from top to bottom. Fasten off.

CROCHETING BACKPACK OPENING

With RS facing, front to your left, and Yarn D, insert hook in rightmost st at left side top, ch 1, sc in same st and in each of next sts along left side, sc in each of next sc along front top edge, sc in each of next sts along right side, sc in each of next unused lps of 1st row of flap. Join with sl st in 1st sc. Fasten off.

CROCHETED BACK STRAP (MAKE 2)

With RS of back facing, bottom close to you, and Yarn D, insert hook in 9th sc (30th sc for 2nd strap) at bottom attaching row, ch 1, sc in same sc and in each of 2 next sc at bottom attaching row.

Rows 1–40: Ch 1, sc in 1st sc from hook and in each of next rem sc—3 sc. Fasten off.

SIDE STRAP (MAKE 2)

With RS of back facing, bottom to your left (right), and Yarn C, insert hook in 1st sc (3rd sc) at side attaching row, ch 1, sc in same sc and in each of 2 next sc at side attaching row.

Rows 1–7: Ch 1, sc in 1st sc from hook and in each of next rem sc—3 sc.

Row 8 (button loop): Ch 4, join with sl st in 1st sc of prev row.

Row 9: Ch 1, 3 sc in the lp. End with sl st in last sc of row 7. Fasten off.

Fold over backpack flap and side straps and sew buttons on backpack front, corresponding to button loops.

Fold over pocket flaps and sew buttons on pocket fronts, corresponding to button loops.

this project was crocheted with

(A) 4 balls of Lion Chenille Thick & Quick, 91% acrylic/9% rayon, super bulky weight, approx 100yd/90m per ball, color #950-124

(B) 1 ball of Lion Chenille Thick & Quick, 91% acrylic/9% rayon, super bulky weight, approx 100yd/90m per ball, color #950-098

(C) 1 ball of Lion Wool-Ease Thick & Quick, 80% acrylic/20% wool, super bulky weight, approx 6oz/170g = approx 106yd/97m per ball, color 640-099

(D) 2 balls of Lion Wool-Ease Thick & Quick, 80% acrylic/20% wool, super bulky weight, approx 6oz/170g = approx 106yd/97m per ball, color 640-404

Straps: HempBasics 51mm (±2") Hemp Webbing

rolled scroll pencil case

This pencil case features spiraled sides, reminiscent of a scrolled sheaf of paper. It's a perfect match for the Classic Campus Backpack (page 40) and just the right size for holding pencils, pens, and other school supplies.

EXPERIENCE LEVEL

■■■☐ Intermediate

FINISHED MEASUREMENTS

- 8½"/21.6cm long x 3"/7.6cm diameter at side

MATERIALS AND TOOLS

- Yarn A **6 SUPER BULKY**: 100yd/90m of Super bulky yarn, acrylic/rayon, white

- Yarn B **6 SUPER BULKY**: 106yd/97m of Super bulky yarn, acrylic/wool, brown

- Yarn C **6 SUPER BULKY**: 106yd/97m of Super bulky yarn, acrylic/wool, cream

- Size H/8 (5mm) crochet hook OR SIZE TO OBTAIN GAUGE

- Straight pins

- Two 2-hole wooden buttons, ¾"/1.9cm diameter

- Sewing needle and thread

- Tapestry needle

GAUGE

With Yarn A, 8 sts and 4 rows = 3"/7.6cm in dc

PATTERN

Chess Pattern: BP dc around each of next 3 dc, FP dc around each of next 3 dc

SPECIAL STITCHES

Front Post Double Crochet Stitch (FP dc) (page 14)

Back Post Double Crochet Stitch (BP dc) (page 15)

instructions

BODY

With Yarn B, ch 22.

Row 1: Ch 1, sc into 2nd ch from hook and in each of next rem chs—22 sc. Cut yarn.

Row 2: Join Yarn A, ch 1, sc into 2nd ch from hook and in each of next rem chs—22 sc.

Row 3: Ch 3, dc in 1st sc from hook and in each of next rem sc—22 dc.

Row 4: Ch 3, FP dc around 2nd dc in prev row and around each of next 2 dc; *BP dc around each of next 3 dc, FP dc around each of next 3 dc. Rep from * 3 times. End with dc in 3rd ch of ch-3 in prev row.

Chess Pattern

Rows 5–15: Ch 3, FP dc around 1st FP dc in prev row and around each of next 2 FP dc; *BP dc around each of next 3 BP dc, FP dc around each of next 3 FP dc. Rep from * 3 times. End with dc in 3rd ch of ch-3 in prev row.

Row 16: Ch 3, FP dc around 1st FP dc in prev row and around each of next 20 FP dc. End with dc in 3rd ch of ch-3 in prev row—21 FP dc.

Row 17: Ch 1, sc in 1st dc and each of next 21 FP dc—22 sc. Fasten off.

ROUND SIDE (MAKE 2)

With Yarn B, ch 4, join with sl st in 1st ch to form a ring.

Rnd 1: Ch 1, 8 sc in ring. Join with sl st in 1st sc.

Rnd 2: Join C, ch 1, 2 sc in same sc as joining and in each rem sc. Join with sl st in 1st sc—16 sc.

Rnd 3: With Yarn B, ch 1, sc in same sc as joining, 2 sc in next sc, *sc in next sc, 2 sc in next sc. Rep from * 7 times. Join with sl st in 1st sc—24 sc. Cut yarn.

Rnd 4: With Yarn C, ch 1, sc in same sc as joining and in each rem sc. Join with sl st in 1st sc—24 sc. Fasten off.

STRAP (MAKE 2)

With Yarn B, ch 26.

Row 1: Ch 3, dc in 4th ch from hook and in each of next rem chs—26 dc. For button loop, turn, 3 sc around last dc in prev row. End with sl st in foundation ch. Fasten off.

SEWING ON STRAPS AND BUTTONS (REP TWICE)

With RS of body and strap facing, last row of body close to you, place strap bottom (end without button loop) 3"/7.6cm from top and 3"/7.6cm from right (left) side of body, and pin. Using Yarn C and tapestry needle, sew on strap bottom with a few sts that are not visible from RS. With button loop close to you, sew button on strap bottom, below seam connecting strap to body.

ATTACHING ROUND SIDES TO BODY

Note: The sides are round and the body is wrapped around them when they are attached. The body will overlap by about 1"/2.5cm to make a covered opening.

With RS of body and WS of round side facing, bottom to your left, and Yarn B, insert hook in rightmost st at side edge of body and in joining st of round side, ch 1, sc in same pair of sts and in each pair along edges. Roll body around side when working. The overlap starts here. Cont with sc in each st at body edge, and each sc of attaching rnd. Join with sl st in next sc of attaching rnd. Fasten off.

With overlapped part facing, attached side close to you, and Yarn B, insert hook in rightmost st at side edge of body, in corresponding st of interior, and in joining st of round side, ch 1, sc in same pair of sts and in each pair along edges. Join with sl st in 1st sc. Fasten off.

this project was crocheted with

(A) 1 ball of Lion Chenille Thick & Quick, 91% acrylic/9% rayon, super bulky weight, approx 100yd/90m per ball, color #950-098

(B) 1 ball of Lion Wool-Ease Thick & Quick, 80% acrylic/20% wool, super bulky weight, approx 6oz/170g = approx 106yd/97m per ball, color 640-404

(C) 1 ball of Lion Wool-Ease Thick & Quick, 80% acrylic/20% wool, super bulky weight, approx 6oz/170g = approx 106yd/97m per ball, color 640-099

parisian floral purse

This cocoon-shaped purse, which features a delicate lace lining and bold bright yarn, is perfectly accompanied by the Pretty Purple Change Purse (page 57). Finish it with a handmade hemp handle (in photo) or use a readymade bamboo or wood handle.

EXPERIENCE LEVEL

■■■□ Intermediate

FINISHED MEASUREMENTS

9½"/24.1cm wide x 10"/25.4cm high

MATERIALS AND TOOLS

Yarn A : 330yd/300m of Bulky weight yarn, nylon, in purple

Yarn B : 332yd/304m of Light weight yarn, acrylic/nylon/polyester, in purple with white

Yarn C: 21.9yd/20m of Thin, 3-strand hemp yarn, in natural beige

Size E/4 (3.5mm) crochet hook OR SIZE TO OBTAIN GAUGE

Lining: Two pieces of reversible beige lace: One rectangle: 13½"/34.2cm wide x 20"/50.8.cm long; One circle: 6"/15.2cm in diameter

Sewing needle and thread

Straight pins

Flexible hemp handle or readymade handle

For flexible hemp handle:

One piece of 18 gauge half-hard round steel wire, 80"/203.2cm long

One piece of 5/32"/4mm natural beige hemp rope, 40"/101.6cm long

Wire cutters

For readymade handle:

One 7"/18cm bamboo or wood handle, with curled ends

GAUGE

With Yarn A, 10 sts and 3 rows = 2"/5cm in dc

SPECIAL STITCHES

Puff Stitch (Puff st) (page 15)

TECHNIQUES

Flexible hemp handle (page 19)

instructions

FLOWER (MAKE 2—1 FOR BOTTOM AND 1 FOR FLEXIBLE HEMP HANDLE)

With Yarn B, ch 8, join with sl st in 1st ch to form a ring.

Rnd 1: Ch 1, 16 sc in ring. Join with sl st in 1st sc.

Rnd 2: Join Yarn A, ch 3, Puff st in same sc as joining, ch 2; *sk next sc, Puff st in next sc, ch 2. Rep from * 7 times. Join with sl st in last ch of beg ch-3—8 Puff sts.

Rnd 3: With Yarn B, ch 3, sc in 1st ch-2 space of prev rnd, ch 5, sc in same ch-2 space; *ch 2, sc in next ch-2 space, ch 5, sc in same ch-2 space. Rep from * 7 times. Join with sl st in 1st ch of beg ch-3.

Rnd 4: Ch 1, sc in same ch as joining, 2 sc in 1st ch-2 space of prev rnd (between 1st ch-3 and sc), sc in next sc, 5 sc in next ch-5 space; *sc in next sc, 2 sc in next ch-2 space, sc in next sc, 5 sc in next ch-5 space. Rep from * 7 times. Join with sl st in 1st sc.

Rnd 5: With Yarn A, ch 1, sc in 1st ch-2 space of rnd 3, ch 2, 5 dc all in next ch-5 space of rnd 3, ch 2 (this makes 1st flower petal); *sc in next ch-2 space of rnd 3, ch 2, 5 dc all in next ch-5 space of rnd 3, ch 2. Rep from * 7 times. Join with sl st in 1st sc—8 petals.

BODY

Note: Continue working on flower for bottom.

Rnd 1: With Yarn B, ch 1, sc in same sc as joining, ch 6; *sc in next sc of prev rnd, ch 6. Rep from * 7 times. Join with sl st in 1st sc

Rnd 2: Ch 1, sc in same sc as joining, 6 sc in 1st ch-6 space of prev rnd; *sc in next sc, 6 sc in next ch-6 space. Rep from * 7 times. Join with sl st in 1st sc.

Rnd 3: With Yarn A, ch 1, sc in same sc as joining, ch 2, 6 dc all in next ch-6 space of rnd 1, ch 2; *sc in next sc of prev rnd, ch 2, 6 dc all in next ch-6 space of rnd 1, ch 2. Rep from * 7 times. Join with sl st in 1st sc.

Rnd 4: With Yarn B, ch 1, sc in same sc as joining, ch 7; *sc in next sc of prev rnd, ch 7. Rep from * 7 times. Join with sl st in 1st sc

Rnd 5: Ch 1, sc in same sc as joining, 7 sc in 1st ch-7 space of prev rnd; *sc in next sc, 7 sc in next ch-7 space. Rep from * 7 times. Join with sl st in 1st sc.

Rnd 6: With Yarn A, ch 1, sc in same sc as joining, ch 2, 7 dc all in next ch-7 space of rnd 4, ch 2; *sc in next sc of prev rnd, ch 2, 7 dc all in next ch-7 space of rnd 4, ch 2. Rep from * 7 times. Join with sl st in 1st sc.

Rnd 7: With Yarn B, ch 1, sc in same sc as joining, ch 8; *sc in next sc of prev rnd, ch 8. Rep from * 7 times. Join with sl st in 1st sc

Rnd 8: Ch 1, sc in same sc as joining, 8 sc in 1st ch-8 space of prev rnd; *sc in next sc, 8 sc in next ch-8 space. Rep from * 7 times. Join with sl st in 1st sc.

Rnd 9: With Yarn A, ch 1, sc in same sc as joining, ch 2, 8 dc all in next ch-8 space of rnd 7, ch 2; *sc in next sc of prev rnd, ch 2, 8 dc all in next ch-8 space of rnd 7, ch 2. Rep from * 7 times. Join with sl st in 1st sc.

Rnd 10: With Yarn B, ch 1, sc in same sc as joining, ch 9; *sc in next sc of prev rnd, ch 9. Rep from * 7 times. Join with sl st in 1st sc

Rnd 11: Ch 1, sc in same sc as joining, 9 sc in 1st ch-9 space of prev rnd; *sc in next sc, 9 sc in next ch-9 space. Rep from * 7 times. Join with sl st in 1st sc.

Rnd 12: With Yarn A, ch 1, sc in same sc as joining, ch 2, 9 dc all in next ch-9 space of rnd 10, ch 2; *sc in next sc of prev rnd, ch 2, 9 dc all in next ch-9 space of rnd 10, ch 2. Rep from * 7 times. Join with sl st in 1st sc.

Rnd 13: With Yarn B, ch 1, sc in same sc as joining, ch 10; *sc in next sc of prev rnd, ch 10. Rep from * 7 times. Join with sl st in 1st sc

Rnd 14: Ch 1, sc in same sc as joining, 10 sc in 1st ch-10 space of prev rnd; *sc in next sc, 10 sc in next ch-10 space. Rep from * 7 times. Join with sl st in 1st sc.

Rnd 15: With Yarn A, ch 1, sc in same sc as joining, ch 2, 10 dc all in next ch-10 space of rnd 13, ch 2; *sc in next sc of prev rnd, ch 2, 10 dc all in next ch-10 space of rnd 13, ch 2. Rep from * 7 times. Join with sl st in 1st sc.

Rnd 16: With Yarn B, ch 1, sc in same sc as joining, ch 11; *sc in next sc of prev rnd, ch 11. Rep from * 7 times. Join with sl st in 1st sc

Rnd 17: Ch 1, sc in same sc as joining, 11 sc in 1st ch-11 space of prev rnd; *sc in next sc, 11 sc in next ch-11 space. Rep from * 7 times. Join with sl st in 1st sc.

Rnd 18: With Yarn A, ch 1, sc in same sc as joining, ch 2, 11 dc all in next ch-11 space of rnd 16, ch 2; *sc in next sc of prev rnd, ch 2, 11 dc all in next ch-11 space of rnd 16, ch 2. Rep from * 7 times. Join with sl st in 1st sc.

Rnd 19: With Yarn B, ch 1, sc in same sc as joining, ch 12; *sc in next sc of prev rnd, ch 12. Rep from * 7 times. Join with sl st in 1st sc

Rnd 20: Ch 1, sc in same sc as joining, 12 sc in 1st ch-12 space of prev rnd; *sc in next sc, 12 sc in next ch-12 space. Rep from * 7 times. Join with sl st in 1st sc.

Rnd 21: With Yarn A, ch 1, sc in same sc as joining, ch 2, 12 dc all in next ch-12 space of rnd 19, ch 2; *sc in next sc of prev rnd, ch 2, 12 dc all in next ch-12 space of rnd 19, ch 2. Rep from * 7 times. Join with sl st in 1st sc.

Rnds 22–39: Rep rows 19, 20 and 21, 6 times. Fasten off.

CYLINDER LINING

Make a ¼"/06.cm seam all around both pieces of lace. With folded edges facing, fold rectangle piece in half widthwise, and sew a side seam ¼"/0.6cm from edge and 2"/5cm from top to form lining body. Place lace circle and bottom of lining body with folded edges tog, and sew a seam all around, ¼"/0.6cm from edge.

With seam edges facing, make a 1½"/3.8cm fold at top of lining. Sew a seam all around body, ½"/1.3cm from top. The area between this seam and lining body top is the track for the ribbon.

RIBBON

With Yarn C, ch 120.

Row 1: Sl st in 2nd ch from hook and in each rem ch. Cut yarn, tie ends, don't hide tails. Insert ribbon into track at top of lining.

Place WS of purse and seamed side of lining tog. With top 2½"/6.4cm of lining extending above top of purse, pin lining and purse tog. Sew tog with a few sts that are not visible from RS of purse at joining place between loop petals at 2nd rnd of loop petals from top.

HANDLE

Make a flexible hemp handle using Yarn C or use a readymade curled handle. If making flexible hemp hand, insert rem 3"/7.6cm of hemp rope into space in middle of flower. Tie an overhand knot in hemp rope to secure flower, and trim ends.

ATTACHING HANDLE

You have 8 loop petals at purse top; 3 loop petals each for front and back, and one loop petal at each side. If you are using a readymade handle, insert curled ends into side loops; if you are using a flexible hemp handle, draw ends of handle through side loops and bend to secure. Shape top of handle as desired.

this project was crocheted with

(A) 3 balls of Lion Incredible, 100% nylon, bulky weight, 1.75oz/50g = approx 110yd/100m per ball, color #520–207

(B) 2 balls of Patons Brilliant, 69% acrylic/19%nylon/ 12%polyester, light weight, 1.75oz/50g = approx 166yd/ 152m per ball, color #-03320

(C) 1 spool of HempBasics, 100% hemp 3-strand yarn, 17.6oz/500g = approx 1800yd/ 1642m per spool

Rope: HempBasics ⁵⁄₃₂"/4mm Natural Beige Hemp Rope

pretty purple coin purse

This pretty little purse is just the right size for storing spare change and keys. It's a perfect match for the Parisian Floral Purse (page 52).

EXPERIENCE LEVEL

■■■□ Intermediate

FINISHED MEASUREMENTS

5½"/14cm wide x 3"/7.6cm high

MATERIALS AND TOOLS

- Yarn A (**SUPER BULKY 6**): 110yd/100m of Bulky weight yarn, nylon, in purple

- Yarn B (**LIGHT 3**): 166yd/152m of Light weight yarn, acrylic/nylon/polyester, in purple with white

- Size E/4 (3.5mm) crochet hook OR SIZE TO OBTAIN GAUGE

- One invisible purple zipper, 6"/15cm long

- Straight pins

- Sewing needle and thread

GAUGE

With Yarn A, 6 sts and 2 rows = 2"/5cm in Puff st

SPECIAL STITCHES

Puff Stitch (Puff st) (Page 15)

instructions

BODY

With Yarn B, ch 8, join with sl st in 1st ch to form a ring.

Rnd 1: Ch 1, 16 sc in ring. Join with sl st in 1st sc.

Rnd 2: Join Yarn A, ch 3, Puff st in same sc as joining, ch 2; *sk next sc, Puff st in next sc, ch 2. Rep from * 7 times. Join with sl st in last ch of beg ch-3—8 Puff sts.

Rnd 3: With Yarn B, ch 1, sc in 1st Puff st of prev rnd, 3 sc in 1st ch-2 space; *sc in next Puff st, 3 sc in next ch-2 space. Rep from * 7 times. Join with sl st in 1st sc—32 sc.

Rnd 4: With Yarn A, ch 3, Puff st in same sc as joining, ch 2; *sk next sc, Puff st in next sc, ch 2. Rep from * 15 times. Join with sl st in last ch of beg ch-3—16 Puff sts.

Rnd 5: With Yarn B, ch 1, sc in 1st Puff st of prev rnd, 3 sc in 1st ch-2 space; *sc in next Puff st, 3 sc in next ch-2 space. Rep from * 15 times. Join with sl st in 1st sc—64 sc.

Rnd 6: With Yarn A, ch 3, Puff st in same sc as joining, ch 2; *sk 3 sc, Puff st in next sc, ch 2. Rep from * 15 times. Join with sl st in last ch of beg ch-3—16 Puff sts.

Rnd 7: With Yarn B, ch 1, sc in 1st Puff st of prev rnd, 3 sc in 1st ch-2 space; *sc in next Puff st, 3 sc in next ch-2 space. Rep from * 15 times. Join with sl st in 1st sc—64 sc. Cut yarn.

Rnds 8–16: Ch 1, sc in same sc as joining and in each rem sc. Join with sl st in 1st sc—64 sc.

Rnd 17: Ch 2, sl st in 1st sc of prev rnd, ch 1; *sl st in next sc, ch 1. Rep from * 63 times. Join with sl st in 1st ch of ch-2 st. Fasten off.

ATTACHING ZIPPER

Note: Joining st of each round is back middle of purse.

With RS facing and bottom close to you, flatten front and back of purse. Place leftmost end of zipper at leftmost end of opening, and draw zipper to rightmost side along 2nd rnd from top of opening. Open zipper and pin each side separately. Sew on with a few hidden sts.

this project was crocheted with

(A) 1 ball of Lion Incredible, 100% nylon, bulky weight, 1.75oz/50g = approx 110yd/100m per ball, color #520–207

(B) 1 ball of Patons Brilliant, 69% acrylic/19%nylon/12%polyester, light weight, 1.75oz/50g = approx 166yd/152m per ball, color #-03320

zigzag clutch

The style of this clutch purse is inspired by vibrant Italian fabrics such as those produced by the Missoni fashion house. For a smaller option with similar lines and colors, see the Zigzag Make-Up Bag (page 65).

EXPERIENCE LEVEL

■■■□ Intermediate

FINISHED MEASUREMENTS

- 11½"/29.2cm wide x 6"/15.2cm high x 1"/2.5cm deep

MATERIALS AND TOOLS

- Yarn A : 144yd/200m of Chunky weight yarn, polyester, in dusty green
- Yarn B : 122yd/100m of Chunky weight yarn, polyester, in olive
- Yarn C : 122yd/100m of Chunky weight yarn, polyester, in light beige
- Yarn D : 122yd/100m of Chunky weight yarn, polyester, in dusty blue
- Yarn E : 122yd/100m of Chunky weight yarn, polyester, in rich brown
- Size E/4 (3.5mm) crochet hook OR SIZE TO OBTAIN GAUGE
- Lining: Beige suede, 12"/30.5cm wide x 19"/48cm long
- Parchment paper
- Pencil
- Scissors
- Leather hole punch, 1/10"/2.5mm hole
- Two burnished copper magnetic snaps, ¾"/1.9cm diameter
- One brown leather lace, 32"/81cm long
- Sewing needle and thread

GAUGE

- With Yarn A, 7 sts and 7 rows = 2"/5cm in sc

PATTERN

Zigzag Pattern: Sc in each of next 7 sc, sk next 2 sc, sc in each of next 7 sc, 3 sc in next sc

instructions

BODY

With Yarn C, ch 52. Cut yarn.

Row 1: Join Yarn A, sc in 2nd ch from hook, sk next ch, sc in each of next 6 chs, 3 sc in next ch; *sc in each of next 7 chs, sk next 2 chs, sc in each of next 7 chs, 3 sc in next ch. Rep from * twice. Cont with sc in each of next 6 chs, sk next ch, sc in last ch—51 sc. Cut yarn.

Row 2: Join Yarn B, sc in 1st sc from hook, sk next sc, sc in each of next 6 sc, 3 sc in next sc; *sc in each of next 7 sc, sk next 2 sc, sc in each of next 7 sc, 3 sc in next sc. Rep from * twice. Cont with sc in each of next 6 sc, sk next sc, sc in last sc. Cut yarn.

Rows 3–41: Work following color diagram as follows:

Row 3: E; Row 4: C; Row 5: B; Row 6: A; Row 7: D; Row 8: A; Row 9: B; Row 10: A; Row 11: E; Row 12: A; Row 13: B; Row 14: A; Row 15: C; Row 16: A; Row 17: B; Row 18: D; Row 19: C; Row 20: B; Row 21: A; Row 22: E; Row 23: A; Row 24: B; Row 25: A; Row 26: D; Row 27: A; Row 28: B; Row 29: A; Row 30: C; Row 31: A; Row 32: B; Row 33: E; Row 34: C; Row 35: B; Row 36: A; Row 37: D; Row 38: A; Row 39: B; Row 40: A; Row 41: E. Fasten off.

LINING

Place parchment paper on work surface and place body on top. Trace body outline onto parchment paper, then cut to make template. Place WS of suede on work surface and place template on top. Trace template onto suede, then cut. Using leather hole punch, punch holes ¼"/0.6cm from edge of suede and ¼"/0.6cm apart, all around suede.

Note: You now have one edge with four zigzag peaks and one edge with three zigzag peaks.

ATTACHING SNAPS

Cut 4 suede circles about ¼"/0.6cm larger in diameter than snap.

With RS facing and edge with 4 peaks up, place top of snap (part with protruding center) 1½"/3.8cm below top of two center peaks. Push snap prongs through lining and suede circle, place washer, and push prongs down.

With RS of body facing and edge with 3 peaks up, place bottom of snap (part with depressed center) above 1st beige zigzag valley, corresponding to top of snap.

ATTACHING LINING TO BODY

Place body and lining with WS tog.

With RS of body facing, bottom to your left, and Yarn C, insert hook in rightmost st at side edge of body, and corresponding hole of lining. Ch 1, sc in same st and in each st and corresponding hole along this edge, from top to bottom; 3 sc in corner; cont with sc in each ch of foundation chs and corresponding holes along bottom, making 3 sc in each peak; 3 sc in the corner; sc in each st and corresponding hole along other edge from bottom to top; 3 sc in corner; sc in each sc and corresponding hole along top, making 3 sc in each peak. Join with sl st in 1st sc. Fasten off.

SIDE (MAKE 2)

With Yarn C, ch 8.

Rnd 1: Ch 1, 5 sc in 2nd ch from hook, sc in each of next 8 chs, 5 sc in last ch. Don't turn. Work along bottom side of foundation chs, sc in unused lps of next 8 chs, join with sl st in 1st sc—26 sc.

ATTACHING SIDE TO BODY (REP TWICE)

Note: The sides are oval and the body is wrapped around them when they are attached.

With RS of body and WS of side facing, bottom to your left (right), and Yarn B, insert hook in front lp of joining st (25th row from top, edge st) at crocheted edge of body and in joining st of side. Pull yarn through, sl st in each of next 25 front lps of sts along body edge and sts along side edge. Join with sl st in 1st sl st. Fasten off.

ATTACHING LEATHER LACE

With purse closed, draw each end of leather lace through crocheted edge and corresponding hole at lining on top of purse. Tie an overhand knot in each lace end and sew with a few simple sts to secure.

this project was crocheted with

(A) 2 balls of Lion Suede, 100% polyester, chunky weight, 3oz/85g = approx 122yd/100m per ball, color #210-177

(B) 1 ball of Lion Suede, 100% polyester, chunky weight, 3oz/85g = approx 122yd/100m per ball, color #210-132

(C) 1 ball of Lion Suede, 100% polyester, chunky weight, 3oz/85g = approx 122yd/100m per ball, color #210-123

(D) 1 ball of Lion Suede, 100% polyester, chunky weight, 3oz/85g = approx 122yd/100m per ball, color #210-110

(E) 1 ball of Lion Suede, 100% polyester, chunky weight, 3oz/85g = approx 122yd/100m per ball, color #210-126

zigzag make-up bag

This suede-lined pouch is roomy enough to hold a few make-up essentials, but small enough to fit comfortably into most purses, handbags, and backpacks. For a purse with similar lines and colors, see the Zigzag Clutch (page 60).

EXPERIENCE LEVEL

■■■☐ Intermediate

FINISHED MEASUREMENTS

6"/15.2cm wide x 4"/10cm high x 1"/2.5cm deep

MATERIALS AND TOOLS

Yarn A **5 BULKY**: 122yd/100m of Chunky weight yarn, polyester, in light beige

Yarn B **5 BULKY**: 122yd/100m of Chunky weight yarn, polyester, in dusty blue

Yarn C **5 BULKY**: 122yd/100m of Chunky weight yarn, polyester, in rich brown

Size E/4 (3.5mm) crochet hook OR SIZE TO OBTAIN GAUGE

Lining: Beige suede, 7½"/19cm wide x 14"/35.6cm long

Parchment paper

Pencil

Scissors

Leather hole punch, 1/10"/2.5mm hole

One brown leather lace, 25"/63.5cm long

GAUGE

With Yarn A, 7 sts and 7 rows = 2"/5cm in sc

PATTERN

Zigzag Pattern: Sc in 1st sc from hook, sk next sc, sc in each of next 10 sc, 3 sc in next sc, sc in each of next 10 sc, sk next sc, sc in last sc

instructions

BODY

With Yarn C, ch 24.

Row 1: Sc in 2nd ch from hook and in next 10 chs, 3 sc in next ch, sc in each of next 11 chs—25 sc. Cut yarn.

Row 2: Join Yarn B, sc in 1st sc from hook, sk next sc, sc in each of next 10 sc, 3 sc in next sc, sc in each of next 10 sc, sk next sc, sc in last sc.

Rows 3–30: Work Row 2, following color diagram.

Row 3: B; Row 4: A; Row 5: B; Rows 6: C; Rows 7–8: A; Rows 9–10: C; Row 11: A; Row 12: C; Rows 13: B; Rows 14–15: A; Rows 16–17: B; Row 18: A; Row 19: B; Row 20: C; Rows 21–22: A; Rows 23–24: C; Row 25: A; Row 26: C; Row 27: B; Rows 28–29: A; Row 30: B. Fasten off.

LINING

Place parchment paper on work surface and place body on top. Trace body outline onto parchment paper, then cut to make template. Place WS of suede on work surface and place template on top. Trace template onto suede, then cut. Using leather hole punch, punch holes ¼"/0.6cm from edge of suede, and ¼"/0.6cm, all around suede.

SIDE (MAKE 2)

With Yarn C, ch 9.

Rnd 1: 5 sc in the 2nd ch from hook, sc in each of next 6 chs, 5 sc in last ch. Don't turn. Work along bottom side of foundation chs, sc in unused lps of next 6 chs, join with sl st in 1st sc—22 sc.

ATTACHING LINING TO BODY

Place body and lining with WS tog.

With RS of body facing, bottom to your right, and Yarn A, insert hook in rightmost st at side edge of body, and corresponding hole of lining. Ch 1, sc in same st and in each st and corresponding hole along this edge from bottom to top; 3 sc in corner; cont with sc in each sc and corresponding hold along top, making 3 sc in peak; 3 sc in corner; sc in each st and corresponding hole along other edge, from top to bottom; 3 sc in corner; sc in each ch of foundation chs and corresponding hole along top, making 3 sc in peak. Join with sl st in 1st sc. Fasten off.

ATTACHING SIDE TO BODY (REP TWICE)

Note: The sides are oval and the body is wrapped around them when they are attached.

With RS of body and WS of side facing, bottom to your right (left), and Yarn C, insert hook in front lp of joining st (21st row from bottom, edge st) at crocheted edge of body, and in joining st of side, pull yarn through, sl st in each of next 21 front lps of sts along body edge and sts along side edge. Join with sl st in 1st sl st. Fasten off.

INSERTING LEATHER LACE

With RS of body facing, insert leather lace in middle of 10th row from top of body and draw out in next row. Draw lace through until ends are even and tie a knot in each end.

this project was crocheted with

(A) 1 ball of Lion Suede, 100% polyester, chunky weight, 3oz/85g = approx 122yd/100m per ball, color #210-123

(B) 1 ball of Lion Suede, 100% polyester, chunky weight, 3oz/85g = approx 122yd/100m per ball, color #210-110

(C) 1 ball of Lion Suede, 100% polyester, chunky weight, 3oz/85g = approx 122yd/100m per ball, color #210-126

rolled sushi purse

Perfect for day or night, the handles on this elegant purse are made from two black lacquer chopsticks. A pretty shell button and soft leather lace are used to secure the purse in style.

EXPERIENCE LEVEL

▰▰▰▱ Intermediate

FINISHED MEASUREMENTS

9"/22.9cm wide x 11"/28cm high

9"/22.9cm wide x 9½"/24.1cm high when folded

MATERIALS AND TOOLS

Yarn A : 330yd/300m of Bulky weight yarn, nylon, in variegated blues

Size H/8 (5mm) crochet hook OR SIZE TO OBTAIN GAUGE

One 2-hole shell button, ¾"/1.9cm diameter

Two black lacquer decorated chopsticks

One black leather lace, 25"/64cm long

Sewing needle and thread

GAUGE

5 sts and 8 rows = 3"/7.6cm in Puff st, ch 1 patt

SPECIAL STITCHES

Puff Stitch (Puff st) (page 15)

TECHNIQUES

Inserting chopstick handles (page 20)

instructions

BODY

With Yarn A, ch 56, join with sl st in 1st ch to form a ring.

Rnd 1: Ch 1, sc in same ch as joining and in each rem ch—56 sc.

Rnd 2: Ch 3, Puff st in same sc as joining, ch 1; *sk next sc, Puff st in next sc, ch 1. Rep from * 27 times. Join with sl st in last ch of beg ch-3—28 Puff sts.

Rnds 3–21: Sl st in 1st ch-1 space of prev rnd (space between 1st and 2nd Puff sts), ch 3, Puff st in same ch-1 space, ch 1; (Puff st, ch 1) all in each of next 27 ch-1 spaces. Join with sl st in last ch of beg ch-3. You now have 28 Puff sts; 13 Puff sts on front, 13 Puff sts on back, and 1 Puff st on border at left and right sides.

FOLDED PART OF BODY (REP TWICE)

Row 1: With RS of front (back) of body facing, bottom close to you, and Yarn A, insert hook in rightmost Puff st in top row of body, ch 3, Puff st in same st, (ch 1, Puff st) all in each of next 12 Puff sts—13 Puff sts.

Row 2: Ch 1, sc in 1st Puff st from hook; *sc in next ch-1 space, sc in next Puff st. Rep from * 12 times—25 sc.

Row 3: Ch 3, Puff st in 1st sc from hook; *ch 1, sk next sc, Puff st in next sc. Rep from * 12 times—13 Puff sts.

Rows 4–9: Rep rows 2—3, 3 times.

INSERTING CHOPSTICKS

Row 10 (WS): Position chopstick horizontally on last row of front (back) with pointed end to the right (left), ch 1 around chopstick, sc tightly in 1st Puff st from hook over chopstick; *sc tightly in next ch-1 space over chopstick, sc tightly in next Puff st over chopstick. Rep from * 12 times—25 sc. Fasten off.

BOTTOM

Note: This technique is used to close the open space at the bottom of the purse.

With RS of back facing, top close to you, and Yarn A, insert hook from RS to WS in space between 2 rightmost Puff sts of back, ch 3, Puff st in same space, ch 1. Yo, insert hook from WS to RS in rightmost space between 2 rightmost Puff sts of front, Puff st in same space, ch 1. *Yo, insert hook from RS to WS in next space between 2 Puff sts of back, Puff st in same space, ch 1. Yo, insert hook from WS to RS in next space between 2 Puff sts of front, Puff st in same space, ch 1. Rep from * 12 times. End with sl st in last Puff st of back. Fasten off.

INSERTING STRAP

Insert leather lace in 1st row of back, from front to back, in space between 6th and 7th Puff st, and draw out through space between 7th and 8th Puff st. Draw lace through until ends are even.

Sew on button in 1st row of front at 7th Puff st.

this project was crocheted with

3 balls of Lion Incredible, 100% nylon, bulky weight, 1.75oz/50g = approx 110yd/100m per ball, color #520–202

snowy vintage handbag

Show off your great grandmother's favorite brooch with this retro-style handbag. With a sparkling silver snowflake and drawstring, it evokes images of fluffy fresh snow and shiny cold icicles.

EXPERIENCE LEVEL

■■■□ Intermediate

FINISHED MEASUREMENTS

6"/15.2cm diameter at bottom x 7½"/19cm high

MATERIALS AND TOOLS

Yarn A **5** BULKY : 246yd/225m of Chunky weight yarn, acrylic/mohair/cotton/metallic polyester, in variegated blue, gray, and silver

Yarn B **4** MEDIUM : 115yd/105m of Worsted weight yarn, acrylic/cupro/polyester, in sparkling dark blue

Yarn C **4** MEDIUM : 115yd/105m of Worsted weight yarn, acrylic/cupro/polyester, in sparkling silver

Size E/4 (3.5mm) crochet hook OR SIZE TO OBTAIN GAUGE

Sewing needle and matching color thread

Place marker

One antique-style silver brooch

GAUGE

With Yarn A, 10 sts and 10 rows = 2"/5cm in sc

SPECIAL STITCHES

Loop Stitch (Loop st) (page 16)

instructions

ROUND BOTTOM

With Yarn B, ch 5, join with sl st in 1st ch to form a ring.

Rnd 1: Ch 1, 6 sc in ring. Join with sl st in 1st sc.

Rnd 2: Join Yarn A, ch 1, 2 sc in same sc as joining and in each rem sc. Join with sl st in 1st sc—12 sc.

Rnd 3: With Yarn B, ch 1, sc in same sc as joining, 2 sc in next sc, *sc in next sc, 2 sc in next sc. Rep from * 5 times. Join with sl st in 1st sc—18 sc.

Rnd 4: With Yarn A, ch 1, sc in same sc as joining and in next sc, 2 sc in next sc, *sc in each of next 2 sc, 2 sc in next sc. Rep from * 5 times. Join with sl st in 1st sc—24 sc.

Rnd 5: With Yarn B, ch 1, sc in same sc as joining and in each of next 2 sc, 2 sc in next sc, *sc in each of next 3 sc, 2 sc in next sc. Rep from * 5 times. Join with sl st in 1st sc—30 sc.

Rnd 6: With Yarn A, ch 1, sc in same sc as joining and in each of next 3 sc, 2 sc in next sc, *sc in each of next 4 sc, 2 sc in next sc. Rep from * 5 times. Join with sl st in 1st sc—36 sc.

Rnd 7: With Yarn B, ch 1, sc in same sc as joining and in each of next 4 sc, 2 sc in next sc, *sc in each of next 5 sc, 2 sc in next sc. Rep from * 5 times. Join with sl st in 1st sc—42 sc.

Rnd 8: With Yarn A, ch 1, sc in same sc as joining and in each of next 5 sc, 2 sc in next sc, *sc in each of next 6 sc, 2 sc in next sc. Rep from * 5 times. Join with sl st in 1st sc—48 sc.

Rnd 9: With Yarn B, ch 1, sc in same sc as joining and in each of next 6 sc, 2 sc in next sc, *sc in each of next 7 sc, 2 sc in next sc. Rep from * 5 times. Join with sl st in 1st sc—54 sc.

Rnd 10: With Yarn A, ch 1, sc in same sc as joining and in each of next 7 sc, 2 sc in next sc, *sc in each of next 8 sc, 2 sc in next sc. Rep from * 5 times. Join with sl st in 1st sc—60 sc.

Rnd 11: With Yarn B, ch 1, sc in same sc as joining and in each of next 8 sc, 2 sc in next sc, *sc in each of next 9 sc, 2 sc in next sc. Rep from * 5 times. Join with sl st in 1st sc—66 sc.

Note: Marked stitches are for attaching snowflake.

Rnd 12: With Yarn A, ch 1, sc in same sc as joining and in each of next 9 sc, 2 sc in next sc, *sc in each of next 10 sc, 2 sc in next sc. Rep from * 5 times. Join with sl st in 1st sc—72 sc. PM on 1st and each following 12th sc.

Rnd 13: With Yarn B, ch 1, sc in same sc as joining and in each of next 10 sc, 2 sc in next sc, *sc in each of next 11 sc, 2 sc in next sc. Rep from * 5 times. Join with sl st in 1st sc—78 sc.

Rnd 14: With Yarn A, ch 1, sc in same sc as joining and in each of next 11 sc, 2 sc in next sc, *sc in each of next 12 sc, 2 sc in next sc. Rep from * 5 times. Join with sl st in 1st sc—84 sc.

Rnd 15: With Yarn B, ch 1, sc in same sc as joining and in each of next 12 sc, 2 sc in next sc, *sc in each of next 13 sc, 2 sc in next sc. Rep from * 5 times. Join with sl st in 1st sc—90 sc. Cut yarn.

Rnd 16: With Yarn A, ch 1, sc in same sc as joining and in each of next 13 sc, 2 sc in next sc, *sc in each of next 14 sc, 2 sc in next sc. Rep from * 5 times. Join with sl st in 1st sc—96 sc.

BODY

Rnds 1–5: Ch 1, sc in same sc as joining and in each rem sc. Join with sl st in 1st sc.

Rnd 6: Join C, ch 1, sc in same sc as joining and in each rem sc. Join with sl st in 1st sc.

Rnd 7: Join Yarn B, ch 1, sc in same sc as joining and in each rem sc. Join with sl st in 1st sc.

Rnd 8: With Yarn C, ch 1, sc in same sc as joining and in each rem sc. Join with sl st in 1st sc.

Rnd 9: With Yarn A, ch 1, Loop st in same sc as joining and in each rem sc. Join with sl st in 1st Loop st—96 Loop sts.

Rnd 10: With Yarn C, ch 1, sc in same Loop st as joining and in each rem Loop st. Join with sl st in 1st sc—96 sc.

Rnd 11: With Yarn A, ch 1, sc in same sc as joining and in each rem sc. Join with sl st in 1st sc.

Rnd 12: With Yarn C, ch 1, sc in same sc as joining and in each rem sc. Join with sl st in 1st sc.

Rnds 13–32: Rep rnds 9–12, 5 times.

Rnds 33–35: Rep rnds 9–11. Cut yarn

Rnds 36–37: Rep rnd 11, twice.

Rnd 38 (ribbon loops): Ch 1, sc in same sc as joining, ch 2, sk next 2 sc, sc in each of next 9 sc; *ch 2, sk next 2 sc, sc in each of next 3 sc, ch 2, sk next 2 sc, sc in each of next 9 sc. Rep from * 5 times, then ch 2, sk next 2 sc, sc in each of next 2 sc. Join with sl st in 1st sc.

Rnd 39: Ch 1, sc in same sc as joining, 2 sc in 1st ch-2 space, sc in each of next 9 sc; *2 sc in next ch-2 space, sc in each of next 3 sc, 2 sc in next ch-2 space, sc in each of next 9 sc. Rep from * 5 times, then 2 sc in next ch-2 space, sc in each of next 2 sc. Join with sl st in 1st sc.

Rnd 40: Rep rnd 11. Cut yarn.

Rnd 41: Join Yarn C, ch 2, sl st in same sc as joining, ch 2; *sl st in next sc, ch 2. Rep from * 95 times. Join with sl st in 1st sl st. Fasten off.

SNOWFLAKE

With Yarn C, ch 6, join with sl st in 1st ch to form a ring.

Rnd 1: Ch 1, 12 sc in ring. Join with sl st in 1st sc.

Rnd 2: Ch 3, 2 dc in same sc as joining, ch 4; *sk next sc, 3 dc in next sc, ch 4. Rep from * 5 times. Join with sl st in last ch of beg ch-3.

Rnd 3: Ch 3, 4 dc in 1st ch-4 space of prev rnd, ch 4; *5 dc in next ch-4 space, ch 4. Rep from * 5 times. Join with sl st in last ch of beg ch-3.

Rnd 4: (Ch 1, sl st) all in 1st dc and in each of next 3 dc of prev rnd, ch 1, (3 sc, ch 9, 3 sc) all in 1st ch-4 space; *(sl st, ch 1) all in each of next 5 dc, (3 sc, ch 9, 3 sc) all in next ch-4 space. Rep from * 5 times. Join with sl st in 1st ch. Fasten off.

Attach snowflake on bag bottom by sewing each ch-9 loop of last row of snowflake to marked sts on bag bottom with a few simple sts.

STRAP

With 2 strands of Yarn A, ch 180.

Rnd 1: Join Yarn C, ch 1, sl st in 2nd ch from hook; *ch 1, sl st in next ch. Rep from * 179 times. Don't turn. Work along bottom side of foundation chs in unused lps of next 180 chs and *ch 1, sl st in next ch. Rep from * 180 times. Fasten off.

Note: Joining st of each round is back middle of purse.

With RS facing and bottom close to you, flatten front and back of purse. At rightmost (leftmost) side, insert one end of strap above 2nd Loop st rnd from top, from back to front. Draw strap through and insert above next Loop st rnd. Draw through from front to back. Fold upwards and sew strap end onto strap.

RIBBON

With Yarn A, ch 120.

Rnd 1: Join Yarn B, ch 1, sl st in 2nd ch from hook and in each of next rem chs. Fasten off.

With RS of front facing and bottom close to you, insert ribbon in hole to right of middle center, weave through each ribbon loop all around, and draw out through last loop.

DAISIES

With Yarn D, insert hook into 2nd ch at one ribbon end, *picot, sc in same ch of ribbon. Rep from * 3 times in front lp of ch st and 2 more time in back lp of same ch. End with sl st in 1st ch from beg rnd. Fasten off.

With Yarn C, insert hook into 2nd ch at other ribbon end and make another daisy.

ATTACHING BROOCH

Attach brooch at front middle of purse, 1½"/3.8cm below ribbon, so that pin of brooch is behind ribbon and front of brooch closes over ribbon.

this project was crocheted with

(A) 3 balls of Lion Moonlight Mohair, 57% acrylic/28% mohair/9% cotton/6% metallic polyester, chunky weight, 1.75oz/50g = approx 82yd/75m per ball, color #510-205

(B) 1 ball of Glitterspun, 60% acrylic/27% cupro/13% polyester, worsted weight, 1.75oz/50g = approx 115yd/105m per ball, color #990-109

(C) 1 ball of Glitterspun, 60% acrylic/27% cupro/13% polyester, worsted weight, 1.75oz/50g = approx 115yd/105m per ball, color #990-150

sun and sea beach bag

With shades of blue and bright yellow, this bag conjures images of a sandy beach on a sunny day. It also features a practical plastic lining that can be wiped clean of salt water and sand. This project is perfectly paired with the Pear Sunglass Holder (page 86).

EXPERIENCE LEVEL

■■■□ Intermediate

FINISHED MEASUREMENTS

13½"/34.3cm wide x 14½"/36.8cm high x 3"/7.6cm deep

MATERIALS AND TOOLS

Yarn A (4 MEDIUM): 120yd/109m of Medium weight yarn, cotton, in white

Yarn B (4 MEDIUM): 240yd/218m of Medium weight yarn, cotton, in variegated blue

Yarn C (4 MEDIUM): 120yd/109m of Medium weight yarn, cotton, in bright yellow

Yarn D (4 MEDIUM): 242yd/2189m of Medium weight yarn, cotton, in deep turquoise

Yarn E (4 MEDIUM): 120yd/109m of Medium weight yarn, cotton, in green

Size E/4 (3.5mm) crochet hook OR SIZE TO OBTAIN GAUGE

Strap: Transparent plastic drawer mat, 3"/7.6cm wide x 40"/101.6cm long

Lining: Transparent plastic drawer mat, 15"/38.1cm wide x 15"/38.1cm long

Parchment paper

Pencil

Scissors

Straight pins

Leather hole punch, ⅒"/2.5mm hole

One silver magnetic snap, ¾"/1.9cm diameter

GAUGE

With Yarn A, 10 sts and 4 rows = 2"/5cm in dc

With Yarn D, 5 sts and 2 rows = 2"/5cm in Popcorn

SPECIAL STITCHES

Picot: Ch 3, sl st in 1st ch of ch-3 (page 17)

Popcorn Stitch (Popcorn): 3 tr in next st, remove hook from lp and insert in ch-2 space, insert into dropped st and draw it through, ch 2 (page 16)

Popcorn1: 3 dc in next st, remove hook from lp and insert in ch-2 space, insert into dropped st and draw it through, ch 2 (page 16)

instructions

FRONT AND BACK

With Yarn A, ch 39.

Row 1: Ch 3, dc in 4th ch from hook and in each of next 37 chs, dc 8 in last ch. Don't turn. Work along bottom side of foundation chs and dc in each of next unused lps of 39 chs—85 dc. Cut yarn.

Row 2: Join Yarn B, ch 6, sk 1st dc from hook, Popcorn in next dc, sk next dc; *Popcorn in next dc, sk next dc. Rep from * 17 times. Make Popcorn in each of next 10 dc, sk next dc; **Popcorn in next dc, sk next dc. Rep from ** 18 times. End with tr in 3rd ch of ch-3 in prev row—46 Popcorns. Cut yarn.

Row 3: Join Yarn C, ch 5, hdc in 1st ch-2 space (space between 2 last Popcorns in prev row); *ch 2, hdc in next ch-2 space. Rep from * 18 times. Ch 1, **(hdc, ch 1, hdc, ch 1) all in next ch-2 space. Rep from ** 7 times. Cont with ***hdc in next ch-2 space, ch 2. Rep from *** 19 times. End with hdc in 4th ch of ch-6 in prev row—53 hdc.

Row 4: Join Yarn D, ch 4, dc in 1st space (space between 2 last hdc in prev row); *ch 1, dc in next space. Rep from * 19 times. Ch 2, **hdc in next space, ch 2. Rep from ** 13 times. Cont with ***dc in next space, ch 1. Rep from *** 20 times. End with dc in 3rd ch of ch-5 in prev row. Cut Yarn D.

Row 5: With Yarn C, ch 5, tr in 1st space (space between 2 last dc in prev row); *ch 1, tr in next space. Rep from * 14 times. Ch 1 and work 2 htr in each of next 6 spaces; 2 dc in each of next 3 spaces; 3 dc in each of next 6 spaces; 2 dc in each of next 3 spaces; 2 htr in each of next 6 spaces. Cont with ch 1, **tr in next space, ch 1. Rep from ** 15 times. End with tr in 3rd ch of ch-4 in prev row. Cut yarn.

Row 6: Join Yarn A, ch 1, sc in 1st tr from hook and in each of next ch-1 spaces and sts in prev row. End with sc in 4th ch of ch-5 in prev row—117 sc. Cut yarn.

Row 7: Join Yarn D, ch 6, sk 1st sc from hook, Popcorn in next sc, sk next sc; *Popcorn in next sc, sk next sc. Rep from * 21 times. Cont with **Popcorn1 in next sc, sk next sc. Rep from ** twice. Work Popcorn1 in each of next 17 sc, sk next sc, then rep from ** twice and from * 22 times. End with tr in 1st sc in prev row. Cut yarn.

Row 8: Join Yarn A, ch 5, hdc in 1st ch-2 space (space between 2 last Popcorns in prev row); *ch 2, hdc in next ch-2 space. Rep from * 24 times. Ch 2, **(hdc, ch 1, hdc) all in next ch-2 space. Rep from ** 14 times. Work * 25 more times, ch 2. End with hdc in 4th ch of ch-6 in prev row—79 hdc. Cut yarn.

Row 9: Join Yarn B, ch 6, Popcorn in 1st ch-2 space (space between 2 last hdc in prev row) and in each of next 21 ch-2 spaces; Popcorn1 in each of next 4 ch-2 spaces; Popcorn1 in each of next 14 ch-1 spaces; Popcorn1 in each of next 4 ch-2 spaces; Popcorn in each of next 22 ch-2 spaces. End with tr in 3rd ch of ch-5 in prev row. Cut yarn.

Row 10: Join Yarn A, ch 5, hdc in 1st ch-2 space (space between 2 last Popcorns in prev row), ch 2; *hdc in next ch-2 space, ch 2. Rep from * 24 times. Cont with **(hdc, ch 1, hdc, ch 1) all in next ch-2 space. Rep from ** 15 times. Ch 1, then work * 25 more times. End with hdc in 4th ch of ch-6 in prev row—81 hdc. Cut yarn.

Row 11: Join Yarn D, ch 6, Popcorn in 1st ch-2 space (space between 2 last hdc in prev row) and in each of next 21 ch-2 spaces; Popcorn1 in each of next 4 ch-2 spaces. Work *Popcorn1 in next ch-1 space, ch 1, sk next ch-1 space. Rep from * 14 times. Popcorn1 in next ch-1 space, then Popcorn1 in each of next 4 ch-2 spaces; Popcorn in each of next 22 ch-2 spaces. End with tr in 3rd ch of ch-5 in prev row. Cut Yarn D.

Rnd 12: Join Yarn A, ch 1, 3 sc in 1st tr from hook, 2 sc in next ch-2 space (space between last tr and Popcorn in prev row) and in each of next 25 ch-2 spaces, 3 sc in each of next 14 ch-3 spaces, 2 sc in each of next 26 ch-2 spaces, 3 sc in 4th ch of ch-5 in prev row. Cont along bottom edge and sc in each 'sc' row, 2 sc in each 'hdc' and 'dc' row, 3 sc in each 'tr' and 'Popcorn' row. Join with sl st in 1st sc—152 sc + 52 sc along bottom. Cut yarn.

Rnd 13: Join Yarn E, ch 1, sc in same sc as joining, 3 sc in next sc, sc in each of next 148 sc, 3 sc in next sc, sc in each of next 53 sc. Join with sl st in 1st sc—208 sc. Fasten off.

STRAP

Plastic part of strap

Cut ends of strap so that they are rounded, with a radius of 1"/2.5cm. Using leather hole punch, punch holes ¼"/0.6cm from edge of strap, and ¼"/0.6cm apart, all around strap. At either end of strap, punch additional holes ¼"/0.6cm apart in a half-circle shape. Arc of the half circle should be ½"/1.3cm from edge, and diameter should be 1"/2.5 from ends. (This will be used later to connect crocheted strap.)

With RS of plastic part facing and Yarn D, insert hook in a corner hole, picot, *sl st in next hole, picot. Rep from * all around plastic part of strap. Join with sl st in 1st ch st. Fasten off.

Crocheted part of strap

With Yarn D, ch 10.

Row 1: Ch 1, sc in 2nd ch from hook and in each of next rem chs—10 sc.

Rows 2–6: Ch 1, sc in 1st sc from hook and in each of next 9 sc—10 sc. Cut yarn.

Rows 7–74: Work Row 2, following color diagram.

Rows 7–8: Yarn C; Rows 9–12: Yarn D; Rows 13–14: Yarn A; Rows 15–16: Yarn E; Rows 17–18: Yarn A; Rows 19–22: Yarn D; Rows 23–24: Yarn C; Rows 25–32: B; Rows 33–34: Yarn A; Rows 35–40: Yarn B; Rows 41–42: Yarn A; Rows 43–50: Yarn B; Rows 51–52: Yarn C; Rows 53–56: Yarn D; Rows 57–58: Yarn A; Rows 59–60: Yarn E; Rows 61–62: Yarn A; Rows 63–66: Yarn D; Rows 67–68: Yarn C; Rows 69–74: Yarn D.

With RS of crocheted part facing, bottom to your left, and Yarn A, insert hook in rightmost st at crocheted part edge, picot, *sk next edge st, sl st in next st, picot. Rep from * all round crocheted part of strap. Join with sl st in 1st ch st. Fasten off.

LINING (MAKE 2)

Place parchment paper on work surface and place front or back on top. Trace outline onto parchment paper then cut to make template. Place WS of plastic on work surface and place template on top. Cut plastic. Using leather hole punch, punch holes ¼"/0.6cm from edge of lining, and ¼"/0.6cm apart, all around lining.

ATTACHING SNAP (REP TWICE)

Cut 2 circles of plastic that are about ¼"/0.6cm larger in diameter than snap.

With RS facing, place one side of snap 2"/5cm down from top middle. Push snap through lining and plastic circle, place washer, and push down prongs.

ATTACHING LINING TO FRONT AND BACK (REP TWICE)

Place front (back) and lining with WS tog.

With RS of front (back) facing and Yarn A, insert hook in joining st at last rnd of front (back) and in corresponding hole at lining, ch 1, sc in same st and in each st and corresponding hole, all around front (back). Join with sl st in 1st sc. Fasten off.

ATTACHING STRAP TO FRONT AND BACK

Note: Plastic part of strap creates sides and bottom of bag.

With RS of front and WS of strap facing, place RS of middle bottom of front (back) on WS of middle of plastic part of strap. Pin along bottom and 12"/30.5cm along each side edge of front (back), leaving curved top open.

With RS of front facing, bottom to your right, and Yarn D, insert hook in rightmost sc of attaching rnd and in corresponding hole on plastic part of strap. Ch 1, sc in next sc and corresponding hole along side of front (back) from bottom to top. Cont with sc in each of next sc of attaching rnd along bag opening. Sc in next sc and corresponding hole along other side of front (back), from top to bottom, and along bottom. Join with sl st in 1st sc. Fasten off.

CROCHETED EDGES OF LOOSE PART OF PLASTIC STRAP (REP TWICE)

With RS of strap facing and Yarn D, insert hook in last connected hole of plastic part of strap before opening, picot, *sl st in next hole, picot. Rep from * all around loose part of plastic strap. End with sl st in next connected hole after opening. Fasten off.

ATTACHING CROCHETED PART TO PLASTIC PART (REP TWICE)

With RS of plastic strap and RS of crocheted strap facing, place one end of plastic strap 1½"/3.8cm over one end of crocheted strap, and pin.

With Yarn C, insert hook in one half-circle hole on plastic strap, and in corresponding place on crocheted strap. Draw yarn through and make overlap chs in next and each hole and corresponding place on crocheted strap all around half-circle. Fasten off.

Rnd 1: With RS of plastic strap facing and Yarn C, insert hook in one of the overlapped chs, picot, *sl st in next overlap ch, picot. Rep from * all round half circle. Join with sl st in 1st ch st. Fasten off.

this project was crocheted with

(A) 1 ball of Lily Sugar'n Cream, 100% cotton, medium weight yarn, 2.5oz/71g = approx 120yd/109m, color #0001

(B) 2 balls of Lily Sugar'n Cream, 100% cotton, medium weight yarn, 2.5oz/71g = approx 120yd/109m, color #02744

(C) 1 ball of Lily Sugar'n Cream, 100% cotton, medium weight yarn, 2.5oz/71g = approx 120yd/109m, color #00073

(D) 2 balls of Lily Sugar'n Cream, 100% cotton, medium weight yarn, 2.5oz/71g = approx 120yd/109m, color #01742

(E) 1 ball of Lily Sugar'n Cream, 100% cotton, medium weight yarn, 2.5oz/71g = approx 120yd/109m, color #01712

Strap and Lining: Ikea Rationell Variera Drawer Mat

pear sunglass holder

Keep your sunglasses on hand (and in style) with this pear-shaped sunglass holder. It features a soft suede interior to keep lenses from getting scratched, and a brightly colored exterior. Tote it along inside the Sun and Sea Beach Bag (page 80) on your next trip to the beach.

EXPERIENCE LEVEL

■■■□ Intermediate

FINISHED MEASUREMENTS

4½"/11.4cm wide x 8"/20.3cm high x ½"/1.3cm deep

MATERIALS AND TOOLS

Yarn A : 120yd/109m of Medium weight yarn, cotton, in white

Yarn B : 120yd/109m of Medium weight yarn, cotton, in variegated blue

Yarn C : 120yd/109m of Medium weight yarn, cotton, in bright yellow

Yarn D : 120yd/109m of Medium weight yarn, cotton, in deep turquoise 120yd/109m of medium weight yarn, cotton, in deep turquoise

Size E/4 (3.5mm) crochet hook OR SIZE TO OBTAIN GAUGE

Strap: Transparent plastic drawer mat, 3"/7.6cm wide x 40"/101.6cm long

Parchment paper

Pencil

Scissors

Lining: Blue suede, 10"/25.4cm wide x 16"/40.6cm long

Leather hole punch, 1/10"/2.5mm hole

Tracing paper

One piece of green suede, 1"/2.5cm wide x 4"/10cm long

One light purple shank button, ¼"/0.6cm diameter

Sewing needle and thread

GAUGE

With Yarn A, 10 sts and 4 rows = 2"/5cm in dc

With Yarn B, 5 sts and 2 rows = 2"/5cm in Popcorn

SPECIAL STITCHES

Picot: Ch 3, sl st in 1st ch of ch-3 (page 17)

Popcorn Stitch (Popcorn): 3 tr in next st, remove hook from lp and insert in ch-2 space, insert into dropped st and draw it through, ch 2 (page 16)

TECHNIQUES

Crocheting single crochet in holes (page 18)

instructions

FRONT AND BACK (MAKE 2)

With Yarn A, ch 16.

Rnd 1: Sc into 2nd ch from hook and in each of next 4 chs, dc in each of next 4 chs, htr in each of next 3 chs, tr in each of next 2 chs, 10 tr in last ch. Don't turn. Work along bottom side of ch in unused lps of next 16 chs, tr in each of next 2 chs, htr in each of next 3 chs, tr in each of next 2 chs, dc in each of next 4 chs, sc in each of next 5 chs, join with sl st in 1st sc. Cut yarn.

Rnd 2: Join Yarn B, ch 4, 2 tr in same sc as joining. Remove hook from lp and insert in space between ch-4 and 1st tr, insert into dropped lp and draw it through, ch 2 (this makes 1st Popcorn), *sk next st, Popcorn in next st. Rep from * 8 times. Sk next st, then make Popcorn in each of next 8 sts, **sk next st, Popcorn in next st. Rep from ** 7 times. Make one more Popcorn into joining st, join with sl st in 4th ch-4 st—25 Popcorns. Cut yarn.

Rnd 3: Join C, ch 4; hdc, ch 1, hdc all in 1st ch-2 space of prev rnd; *ch 2, dc in next ch-2 space. Rep from * 7 times. **ch 1, hdc, ch 1, hdc all in next ch-2 space. Rep from ** 9 times. ***Ch 2, hdc in next ch-2 space. Rep from *** 8 times. Ch 2, join with sl st in 3rd ch-4 st. Don't cut yarn.

Rnd 4: Join Yarn D, sl st into space between ch-4 and 1st hdc of prev rnd and ch 4, htr in same space. *Ch 1 and tr. Rep from * 3 times all in next ch-1 space. Ch 2, dc in next space; ch 2, hdc in next space; ch 2, sc in next space; ch 2 sl st in next space; ch 2, sc in next space; ch 2, hdc in next space; ch 2, dc in next space. **Ch 1, dc in next space. Rep from ** 19 times. ***Ch 2 and hdc in next space. Rep from *** 8 times. Ch 2, join with sl st in 3rd ch-4 st. Cut yarn.

Rnd 5: With Yarn C, sl st into space between ch-4 and 1st htr of prev rnd and ch 4, htr in same space; 2 htr in next space; 3 tr and htr all in next space; htr and dc all in next space. *Ch 2, sc in next space. Rep from * 3 times. Ch 2, sl st in next space. **Ch 2, sc in next space. Rep from ** 4 times. Ch 1, hdc in next space; dc and htr all in next space;

2 htr in next space; 3 htr in next space; 2 htr in each of next 3 spaces; 3 htr in each of next 5 spaces; 2 htr in each of next 5 spaces; ch 1, htr in next space; ch 1, dc in next space. ***Ch 2, hdc in next space. Rep from *** 8 times. Ch 2, join with sl st in 3rd ch-4 st. Cut yarn.

Rnd 6 (for back only): With WS of back facing and Yarn A, insert hook in front lp of last rnd joining st, picot, sk next st; *sl st in front lp of next st, picot, sk next st. Rep from * all round. Join with sl st in 1st ch from beg of rnd. Fasten off.

LINING FRONT AND BACK (MAKE 2)

Place parchment paper on work surface and place front on top. Trace outline onto parchment paper then cut to make template. Place WS of blue suede on work surface and place template on top (turn template over to make lining back). Trace template onto suede, then cut. Using leather hole punch, punch holes ¼"/0.6cm from edge of suede and ¼"/0.6cm apart, all around lining.

ATTACHING LINING FRONT AND BACK

Place lining front and back with RS tog. With WS of lining front facing, peak to your right, and Yarn B, insert hook in hole 2½"/6.4cm left of peak and in corresponding hole in back lining, ch 1, sc in same pair of holes, and in every pair around lining until 2"/5cm right of peak. Cont to work around lining front to form an opening. Picot, sk next hole of lining front, *sl st in next hole, picot, sk next hole of lining front. Rep from * until last hole of lining front. End with sl st in 1st ch from beg of rnd.

With RS of lining back facing, peak to your left, and Yarn B, insert hook in 1st hole of opening of lining back. *Picot, sk next hole of lining back; sl st in next hole. Rep from * until peak. Ch 8 to make button lp, sl st in same hole, picot, sk next hole of lining back, *sl st in next hole, picot, sk next hole of lining back. Rep from * until last hole of lining back. End with sl st in 1st ch from beg of rnd. Fasten off.

SIDE

With RS of back facing and Yarn D, insert hook in unused lp of 5th rnd joining st, ch 2, hdc in unused lp of next st, and in each of next unused lps of rem sts all around. Join with sl st in 2nd ch-2 st. Fasten off.

ATTACHING FRONT AND BACK

Note: Since front and back are asymmetrical pear shapes, WS of back becomes RS of holder back when front and back are attached.

Place WS of front with RS of back tog. With RS of front facing, peak to your right, and Yarn A, insert hook in front lp of last rnd 1st sl st of front (about 2½"/6.4cm left of peak), and in back lp of corresponding hdc in side. *Picot, sk next st in both front and side, sl st in front lp of next st in front and in back lp of next hdc in side. Rep from * 38 times (until you are about 2"/5cm right of peak). Cont working around front only to form peak opening. Picot, sk next st; *sl st in front lp of next st, picot, sk next st. Rep from * 11 times. Join with sl st in 1st ch from beg of rnd. Fasten off.

Insert lining into sunglass holder with back of lining corresponding to back of holder. Sew lining and holder tog with a few simple st that are not visible from RS, at beg of opening and at front and back peaks.

ATTACHING LEAF AND BUTTON

Copy leaf template onto tracing paper, then cut out. Place WS of green suede on work surface and place template on top. Trace template onto suede, then cut. Position leaf on sunglass holder so that thinner end of leaf extends above top of front peak. Place button on leaf, just below crocheted edge of sunglass holder front, and sew on button and leaf.

Leaf template

this project was crocheted with

(A) 1 ball of Lily Sugar'n Cream, 100% cotton, medium weight yarn, 2.5oz/71g = approx 120yd/109m, color #0001

(B) 1 ball of Lily Sugar'n Cream, 100% cotton, medium weight yarn, 2.5oz/71g = approx 120yd/109m, color #02744

(C) 1 ball of Lily Sugar'n Cream, 100% cotton, medium weight yarn, 2.5oz/71g = approx 120yd/109m, color #00073

(D) 1 ball of Lily Sugar'n Cream, 100% cotton, medium weight yarn, 2.5oz/71g = approx 120yd/109m, color #01742

brightly striped fringed bottle holder

With horizontal waves of brightly colored yarn, this attractive water bottle holder is extraordinarily practical. It fits a bottle with a 4"/10cm diameter. The height can be adjusted to fit taller bottles.

EXPERIENCE LEVEL

■■■□ Intermediate

FINISHED MEASUREMENTS

4"/10cm in diameter x 9½"/24.1cm high (without cover); 10½"/26.7cm high (with cover)

MATERIALS AND TOOLS

Yarn A : 80yd/73m of knitting Worsted weight yarn, cotton, in hot orange

Yarn B (4) : 80yd/73m of knitting Worsted weight yarn, cotton, in hot green

Yarn C (4) : 80yd/73m of knitting Worsted weight yarn, cotton, in hot pink

Yarn D (4) : 80yd/73m of knitting Worsted weight yarn, cotton, in hot blue

Size E/4 (3.5mm) crochet hook OR SIZE TO OBTAIN GAUGE

Two orange suede discs: One 4"/10cm diameter, and one 2"/5cm diameter

Leather hole punch, ¹⁄₁₀"/2.5mm hole

Sewing needle and matching color thread

One brown leather lace, 30"/76.2cm long

One black leather belt with buckle, ¾"/1.9cm to 1"/2.5cm wide

GAUGE

With Yarn A, 9 sts and 8 rows = 2"/5cm in sc

PATTERN

Wave Pattern: Row 1: Hdc in each of next 2 hdc, dc in each of next 3 sc, hdc in each of next 2 hdc, sc in each of next 3 dc.

Row 2: Hdc in each of next 2 hdc, sc in each of next 3 dc, hdc in each of next 2 hdc, dc in each of next 3 sc

TECHNIQUES

Crocheting single crochet in holes (page 18)

Fringes (page 18)

instructions

BODY

With Yarn B, ch 50, join with sl st in 1st ch to form a ring.

Rnd 1: Ch 3, hdc in 2nd ch of foundation chs, sc in each of next 3 chs, hdc in each of next 2 chs, dc in each of next 3 chs; *hdc in each of next 2 chs, sc in each of next 3 chs, hdc in each of next 2 chs, dc in each of next 3 chs. Rep from * 4 times. Join with sl st in 3rd ch of beg ch-3. Cut yarn.

Wave Pattern

Rnd 2: Join C, ch 3, hdc in 1st hdc of prev rnd, dc in each of next 3 sc, hdc in each of next 2 hdc, sc in each of next 3 dc; *hdc in each of next 2 hdc, dc in each of next 3 sc, hdc

in each of next 2 hdc, sc in each of next 3 dc. Rep from * 4 times. Join with sl st in 3rd ch of beg ch-3. Cut yarn.

Rnd 3: Join Yarn A, ch 3, hdc in 1st hdc of prev rnd, sc in each of next 3 dc, hdc in each of next 2 hdc, dc in each of next 3 sc; *hdc in each of next 2 hdc, sc in each of next 3 dc, hdc in each of next 2 hdc, dc in each of next 3 sc. Rep from * 4 times. Join with sl st in 3rd ch of beg ch-3. Cut yarn.

Rnd 4: Join Yarn D and rep rnd 2.

Rnd 5: Rep rnd 3.

Rnd 6: Join Yarn C and rep rnd 2.

Rnd 7: Join Yarn B and rep rnd 3.

Rnds 8–25: Rep rnds 2–7, 3 times (or to fit bottle)

Rnd 26: Join Yarn C and rep rnd 2.

Rnd 27: Rep rnd 3.

Rnd 28: Join Yarn D and rep rnd 2.

Rnd 29: Rep rnd 3.

Rnd 30: Join Yarn C and rep rnd 2.

Rnd 31: Join Yarn B, ch 4, sk 1st hdc of prev rnd, hdc in next st, ch 1, sk next st; *hdc in next st, ch 1, sk next st. Rep from * 23 times. Join with sl st in 3rd ch of beg ch-4. Cut yarn.

Rnd 32 (loops for leather lace): Join Yarn C, ch 1, 2 sc into space between ch-4 and 1st hdc of prev rnd, 2 sc in each of next ch-1 spaces. Join with sl st in 1st sc—50 sc. Cut yarn.

With WS of body facing, tie overhand knot in ends of each row. Bring yarn ends to RS and trim to 1"/2.5cm.

SUEDE BOTTOM AND TOP

Using leather hole punch, punch holes all around both suede discs, ¼"/0.6cm from edge and ¼"/0.6cm apart.

ATTACHING SUEDE BOTTOM

Note: You may have more sts than holes. If this occurs, you will have to occasionally sk next st, and insert hook in following st and its corresponding hole.

With RS of body and WS of bigger suede disc facing, bottom away from you, and Yarn C, insert hook in joining st of 1st rnd of body and one hole in suede disc. Ch 1, sc in same st and hole, and sc in each of next foundation chs around body bottom and corresponding holes in suede disc. Join with sl st in 1st sc. Fasten off.

COVER

Note: If you have exactly 20 holes, follow instructions below for Rnd 1. If you have more holes, make sc instead of 2 sc in some holes. If you have fewer holes, make 2 sc instead of sc in some holes. It is important to finish with 30 sc.

Rnd 1: With RS of smaller suede disc facing and Yarn C, insert hook in a hole in disc, ch 1, sc in same hole, 2 sc in next hole; *sc in next hole, 2 sc in next hole.

Rep from * 9 times. Join with sl st in 1st sc—30 sc.

Rnd 2: Ch 3, hdc in 2nd sc from hook, sc in each of next 3 sc, hdc in each of next 2 sc, dc in each of next 3 sc; *hdc in each of next 2 sc, sc in each of next 3 sc, hdc in each of next 2 sc, dc in each of next 3 sc. Rep from * twice. Join with sl st in 3rd ch of beg ch-3. Cut yarn.

Rnd 2: Join Yarn B, ch 3, hdc in 1st hdc of prev rnd, dc in each of next 3 sc, hdc in each of next 2 hdc, sc in each of next 3 dc; *hdc in each of next 2 hdc, dc in each of next 3 sc, hdc in each of next 2 hdc, sc in each of next 3 dc. Rep from * twice. Join with sl st in 3rd ch of beg ch-3. Cut yarn.

Rnd 3: Join Yarn C, ch 3, hdc in 1st hdc of prev rnd, sc in each of next 3 dc, hdc in each of next 2 hdc, dc in each of

next 3 sc; *hdc in each of next 2 hdc, sc in each of next 3 dc, hdc in each of next 2 hdc, dc in each of next 3 sc. Rep from * twice. Join with sl st in 3rd ch of beg ch-3. Cut yarn.

Rnd 4: Join Yarn A, ch 1, sc in same st as joining and in each of next 14 sts, ch 6, sc in next st to form loop for leather lace, sc in each of next 14 sts. Join with sl st in 1st sc—30 sc. Fasten off.

BELT HOLDERS (MAKE 4)

With Yarn A, ch 8.

Row 1: Ch 1, sc into 2nd ch from hook and in each of next rem chs—8 sc.

Row 2: Ch 1, sc into 1st sc from hook and in each of next rem sc—8 sc. Fasten off.

FRINGES

With RS of bottle holder facing and bottom away, insert hook in st at attaching suede bottom rnd and make a fringe. Using alternating yarns, rep all around attaching bottom rnd.

With RS of cover facing and top close to you, insert hook in st at last rnd of cover and make a fringe. Using alternating yarns, rep all around, skipping loop for leather lace.

Place cover with last rnd joining st matching same st on bottle holder body, right below loops for holding leather lace, and sew on with a few simple sts.

ATTACHING BELT HOLDERS

With RS facing and bottom close to you, flatten body of bottle holder so that joining stitch is at back middle. Position belt holders horizontally at each side of body, 2"/5cm from top (bottom) of body. Using Yarn C, sew on holders by making an X at either end of each holder.

Insert belt top into top belt holder and draw downwards into bottom holder. Wrap belt around bottom of bottle holder, then insert through bottom and top belt holders on other side. Adjust belt to appropriate length and close.

ATTACHING LEATHER LACE

Insert leather lace in leather lace loop at front middle of bottle holder, from front to back. Draw lace all around bottle holder, weaving it through leather lace loops. Pull out at front middle until lace ends are even. String lace ends through loop on cover, from back to front, then tie an overhand knot at each end.

this project was crocheted with

(A) 1 ball of Bernat Handicrafter Cotton, 100% cotton, medium weight, 1.75oz/50g = approx 80yd/73m per ball, color #13628

(B) 1 ball of Bernat Handicrafter Cotton, 100% cotton, medium weight, 1.75oz/50g = approx 80yd/73m per ball, color #13712

(C) 1 ball of Bernat Handicrafter Cotton, 100% cotton, medium weight, 1.75oz/50g = approx 80yd/73m per ball, color #13740

(D) 1 ball of Bernat Handicrafter Cotton, 100% cotton, medium weight, 1.75oz/50g = approx 80yd/73m per ball, color #13742

hands-free hiking pouch

This sturdy pouch is perfect for holding a wallet, keys, and a granola bar or two. Wear it the next time you go for a walk, and want to keep your hands free. For a smaller version, see the Hands-Free Phone Pouch (page 101).

EXPERIENCE LEVEL

■■■□ Intermediate

FINISHED MEASUREMENTS

10"/25.4cm wide x 9"/22.9cm high x 1"/2.5cm deep

MATERIALS AND TOOLS

Yarn A **SUPER BULKY 6**: 212yd/194m of Super bulky yarn, acrylic/wool, in mixed blue and black

Yarn B **SUPER BULKY 6**: 106yd/97m of Super bulky yarn, acrylic/wool, in blue

Yarn C **SUPER BULKY 6**: 106yd/97m of Super bulky yarn, acrylic/wool, in light brown

Yarn D **SUPER BULKY 6**: 106yd/97m of Super bulky yarn, acrylic/wool, in green

Size K/10½ (6.5mm) crochet hook OR SIZE TO OBTAIN GAUGE

Two old-fashioned shank buttons, 1"/2.5cm diameter

Sewing needle and thread

One silver magnetic snap, ¾"/1.9cm diameter

One leather belt

GAUGE

With Yarn A, 9 sts and 9 rows = 3"/7.6cm in sc

TECHNIQUES

Attaching snap top using crocheted circles for backing (page 20)

SEWING STITCHES

Whip stitch (page 21)

instructions

Note: Since front does not entirely cover back in this project, WS of back is sometimes visible from front. This is referred to as WS of back.

BACK

With Yarn A, ch 24.

Row 1: Ch 1, sc into 2nd ch from hook and in each of next rem chs—24 sc.

Row 2: Ch 1, sc in 1st sc from hook, 2 sc in next sc, sc in each of next 20 sc, 2 sc in next sc, sc in next sc—26 sc.

Row 3: Ch 1, sc in 1st sc from hook and in each of next rem sc—26 sc.

Row 4: Ch 1, sc in 1st sc from hook, 2 sc in next sc, sc in each of next 22 sc, 2 sc in next sc, sc in next sc—28 sc.

Rows 5–7: Ch 1, sc in 1st sc from hook and in each of next rem sc—28 sc.

Row 8: Ch 1, sc in 1st sc from hook, sk next sc, sc in each of next 24 sc, sk next sc, sc in next sc—26 sc.

Row 9: Ch 1, sc in 1st sc from hook and in each of next rem sc—26 sc.

Row 10: Ch 1, sc in 1st sc from hook, sk next sc, sc in each of next 22 sc, sk next sc, sc in next sc—24 sc.

Row 11: Ch 1, sc in 1st sc from hook and in each of next rem sc—24 sc.

Row 12: Ch 1, sc in 1st sc from hook, sk next sc, sc in each of next 20 sc, sk next sc, sc in next sc—22 sc.

Row 13: Ch 1, sc in 1st sc from hook and in each of next rem sc—22 sc.

Row 14: Ch 1, sc in 1st sc from hook, sk next sc, sc in each of next 18 sc, sk next sc, sc in next sc—20 sc.

Rows 15–24: Ch 1, sc in 1st sc from hook and in each of next rem sc—20 sc.

Row 25: Ch 1, sc in 1st sc from hook and in each of next 2 sc, sk next sc, sc in each of next 12 sc, sk next sc, sc in each of next 3 sc—18 sc. Cut yarn.

BELT LOOPS (MAKE 2)

Rows 1–17: With RS of back facing, bottom close to you, and Yarn A, insert hook in rightmost sc (3rd sc from the left for other loop) in last back row, ch 1, sc in 1st sc from hook and in each of next 2 sc—3 sc.

Row 18: Ch 1, sc in 1st sc from hook, ch 2 for buttonhole, sc in next sc.

Row 19: Ch 1, sc in 1st sc from hook, 2 sc in ch-2 space, sc in next sc—4 sc.

Row 20: Ch 1, sc in 1st sc from hook and in each of next rem sc—4 sc. Fasten off.

SIDES AND BOTTOM

Side and bottom foundation

With WS of back facing, bottom to your left, and Yarn B, insert hook in 21st row 2nd st. Work 20 overlay chs along left side of back, from top to bottom, inserting hook in each next row 2nd st (you will now be at 1st row 2nd st). With back bottom close to you, work another 20 overlay chs along back bottom, inserting hook in each next st of 1st row (you will now be at 1st row 22nd st). With back bottom to your right, work 20 more overlay chs along right side of back, from bottom to top, inserting hook in each next row 2nd st from end (you will now be at 21st row 2nd st from end). Cut yarn.

Sides and bottom

Row 1: With Yarn B, insert hook in 1st overlay ch of side foundation, ch 1, sc in same st and in each of next rem

overlay chs across side foundation—60 sc.

Row 2: Ch 1, sc in 1st sc from hook and in each of next rem sc—60 sc.

Row 3: Ch 1, inserting hook in front lp only, sc in 1st sc from hook and in each of next rem sc—60 sc. Fasten off. You now have 60 sc; 20 sc for each side, and 20 sc for the bottom.

INTERIOR DIVIDER

Row 1: With WS of back facing, bottom close to you, and Yarn C, insert hook in back lp of rightmost sc in 2nd row of bottom, ch 1, sc in same lp and in each back lp of next 20 sc along bottom—20 sc.

Row 2: Ch 1, sc in 1st sc from hook, 2 sc in next sc, sc in each of next 16 sc, 2 sc in next sc, sc in next sc—22 sc.

Rows 3–5: Ch 1, sc in 1st sc from hook and in each of next rem sc—22 sc.

Row 6: Ch 1, sc in 1st sc from hook, sk next sc, sc in each of next 18 sc, sk next sc, sc in next sc—20 sc.

Row 7: Ch 1, sc in 1st sc from hook and in each of next rem sc—20 sc.

Row 8: Ch 1, sc in 1st sc from hook, sk next sc, sc in each of next 16 sc, sk next sc, sc in next sc—18 sc.

Row 9: Ch 1, sc in 1st sc from hook and in each of next rem sc—18 sc.

Row 10: Ch 1, sc in 1st sc from hook, sk next sc, sc in each of next 14 sc, sk next sc, sc in next sc—16 sc.

Row 11: Ch 1, sc in 1st sc from hook and in each of next rem sc—16 sc.

Row 12: Ch 1, sc in 1st sc from hook, sk next sc, sc in each of next 12 sc, sk next sc, sc in next sc—14 sc.

Rows 13–19: Ch 1, sc in 1st sc from hook and in each of next rem sc—14 sc. Fasten off.

SEWING ON INTERIOR DIVIDER (REP TWICE)

Fold up interior divider and align with 2nd row of sides. With WS of back facing and bottom to your right (left), sew interior divider to back lps of 2nd row of side with whip sts.

FRONT

Row 1: With WS of back facing, bottom close to you, and Yarn A, insert hook in back lp of rightmost sc in last row of bottom (21st or 40th sc), ch 1, sc in same lp and in each back lp of next 19 sc along bottom—20 sc.

Rows 2–19: Rep rows 2–21 of interior divider. Fasten off.

FLAP

With RS of front facing, bottom close to you, and Yarn B, insert hook in 21st row 3rd st. Work 16 overlay chs along back top, inserting hook in each next st of 21st row. Cut yarn.

Row 1: With RS of front facing, bottom close to you, and Yarn B, insert hook in 1st overlay ch of flap foundation, ch 1, sc in same st and in each of next rem overlay chs along flap foundation—16 sc.

Rows 2–4: Ch 1, sc in 1st sc from hook and in each of next rem sc—16 sc.

Row 5: Ch 1, sc in 1st sc from hook, 2 sc in next sc, sc in each of next 12 sc, 2 sc in next sc, sc in next sc—18 sc.

Row 6: Ch 1, sc in 1st sc from hook and in each of next rem sc—18 sc.

Row 7: Ch 1, sc in 1st sc from hook, 2 sc in next sc, sc in each of next 14 sc, 2 sc in next sc, sc in next sc—20 sc.

Rows 8–10: Ch 1, sc in 1st sc from hook and in each of next rem sc—20 sc.

Row 11: Ch 1, sc in 1st sc from hook, sk next sc, sc in each of next 16 sc, sk next sc, sc in next sc—18 sc.

Row 12: Ch 1, sc in 1st sc from hook and in each of next rem sc—18 sc.

Row 13: Ch 1, sc in 1st sc from hook, sk next sc, sc in each of next 14 sc, sk next sc, sc in next sc—16 sc.

Row 14: Ch 1, sc in 1st sc from hook and in each of next rem sc—16 sc.

Row 15: Ch 1, sc in 1st sc from hook, sk next sc, sc in each of next 12 sc, sk next sc, sc in next sc—14 sc. Fasten off.

ATTACHING FRONT TO SIDES

With RS of front facing, bottom to your left, and Yarn D, insert hook in 1st st at right edge in last row of front and back lp of 1st sc in last row of right side, ch 1, sc in same pair of sts, sc in each of next 18 pairs along right side, from top to bottom, 3 sc in back lp of next sc in last row of right side, sc in unused lps of next 20 sc along bottom, 3 sc in back lp of next sc in last row of left side, sc in 1st st at left edge in 1st row of front and in back lp of next sc in last row of left side, sc in each of next 18 pairs along left side, from bottom to top. Cont and sc in each of next sc along front top. End with sl st in 1st sc. Fasten off.

CROCHETING FLAP EDGES

With RS of front facing, bottom to your left, and Yarn D, insert hook in 1st st at right edge in 1st row of flap, ch 1, sc in same st and in each of next sts along right edge of flap from bottom to top, 3 sc in corner st, sc in each of next sc in last row of flap, 3 sc in corner st, sc in each of next 1st sts along left edge of pocket flap, from top to bottom. Fasten off.

CROCHETING BACK EDGES

With WS of back facing, bottom to your left, and Yarn D, insert hook in 1st st at right edge in last row of back, ch 1, sc in same st and in each of next sts along right edge of back, from top to bottom, 3 sc in corner st, sc in each of

next ch of foundation chs, 3 sc in corner st, sc in each of next 1st sts along left edge of back from bottom to top. Fasten off.

CROCHETING LOOPS AND TOP OF BACK

With RS of back facing, bottom to your right, and Yarn D, insert hook in 1st st at right edge in 1st row of right loop, ch 1, sc in same st and in each of next sts along right edge of right loop from bottom to top, 3 sc in corner st, sc in each of next sc in last row of right loop, 3 sc in corner st, sc in each of next 1st sts along left edge of right loop, from top to bottom; sc in each of next sc in last row of back; sc in each of next 1st sts along right edge of left loop from bottom to top, 3 sc in corner st, sc in each of next sc in last row of left loop, 3 sc in corner st, sc in each of next 1st sts along left edge of left loop, from top to bottom. Fasten off.

SEWING ON BUTTONS

With WS of back facing, sew on buttons on last row of back, corresponding to buttonholes on belt loops when belt loops are folded.

ATTACHING SNAP

Crocheted circle (Make 2)

Note: These crocheted circles provide backing for top and bottom of snap.

With Yarn B, ch 4, join with sl st in 1st ch to form a ring.

Rnd 1: Ch 1, 6 sc in ring. Join with sl st in 1st sc. Fasten off.

Attaching snap bottom

With RS of front facing, bottom close to you, and Yarn B, position bottom of snap (part with inverted center) 3½"/8.9cm in diameter from top and in middle. Push snap prongs through, place washer, and push prongs down. With WS of front facing, place one crocheted circle over snap and sew around with embroidery overlay chs that are not visible on RS of front.

Attaching snap top

With RS of rem circle facing, push top of snap (part with protruding center) prongs through, place washer, and push prongs down. With WS of flap facing, position circle with snap top in corresponding place to bottom of snap. Sew on with whip sts that are not visible on RS of flap.

INSERTING BELT

Button up belt loops and draw belt through.

this project was crocheted with

(A) 2 balls of Lion Wool-Ease Thick & Quick, 80% acrylic/20% wool, super bulky weight, approx 6oz/170g = approx 106yd/97m per ball, color 640-194

(B) 1 ball of Lion Wool-Ease Thick & Quick, 80% acrylic/20% wool, super bulky weight, approx 6oz/170g = approx 106yd/97m per ball, color 640-114

(C) 1 ball of Lion Wool-Ease Thick & Quick, 80% acrylic/20% wool, super bulky weight, approx 6oz/170g = approx 106yd/97m per ball, color 640-1125

(D) 1 ball of Lion Wool-Ease Thick & Quick, 80% acrylic/20% wool, super bulky weight, approx 6oz/170g = approx 106yd/97m per ball, color 640-131

hands-free phone pouch

This handy pouch is just the right size for holding a mobile telephone. It fits on belts of almost any width and is just right for a hike in the forest or stroll through the park. For a larger version, see the Hands-Free Hiking Pouch (page 95).

EXPERIENCE LEVEL

■■□□ Easy

FINISHED MEASUREMENTS

5"/12.7cm wide x 5"/12.7cm high x ½"/1.3cm deep

MATERIALS AND TOOLS

Yarn A : 106yd/97m of Super bulky yarn, acrylic/wool, in mixed blue and black

Yarn B : 106yd/97m of Super bulky yarn, acrylic/wool, in blue

Yarn C : 106yd/97m of Super bulky yarn, acrylic/wool, in green

Size K/10½ (6.5mm) crochet hook OR SIZE TO OBTAIN GAUGE

One old-fashioned brown shank button, 1"/2.5cm diameter

Sewing needle and thread

Leather belt

GAUGE

With Yarn A, 9 sts and 9 rows = 3"/7.6 in sc

instructions

Note: Since front does not entirely cover back in this project, WS of back is sometimes visible from front. This is referred to as WS of back.

BACK

With Yarn A, ch 9.

Row 1: Ch 1, sc into 2nd ch from hook and in each of next rem chs—9 sc.

Rows 2: Ch 1, sc in 1st sc from hook, 2 sc in next sc, sc in each of next 5 sc, 2 sc in next sc, sc in next sc—11 sc.

Row 3: Ch 1, sc in 1st sc from hook and in each of next rem sc—11 sc.

Row 4: Ch 1, sc in 1st sc from hook, 2 sc in next sc, sc in each of next 7 sc, 2 sc in next sc, sc in next sc—13 sc.

Rows 5–7: Ch 1, sc in 1st sc from hook and in each of next rem sc—13 sc.

Row 8: Ch 1, sc in 1st sc from hook, sk next sc, sc in each of next 9 sc, sk next sc, sc in next sc—11 sc.

Row 9: Ch 1, sc in 1st sc from hook and in each of next rem sc—11 sc.

Row 10: Ch 1, sc in 1st sc from hook, sk next sc, sc in each of next 7 sc, sk next sc, sc in next sc—9 sc.

Row 11: Ch 1, sc in 1st sc from hook and in each of next rem sc—9 sc.

Row 12: Ch 1, sc in 1st sc from hook, sk next sc, sc in each of next 5 sc, sk next sc, sc in next sc—7 sc.

Row 13: Ch 1, sc in 1st sc from hook and in each of next rem sc—7 sc.

Row 14: Ch 1, sc in 1st sc from hook, sk next sc, sc in each of next 3 sc, sk next sc, sc in next sc—5 sc.

Row 15: Ch 1, sc in 1st sc from hook and in each of next rem sc—5 sc.

Row 16: Ch 1, sc in 1st sc from hook, sk next sc, sc in next sc, sk next sc, sc in next sc—3 sc.

BELT LOOP

Rows 1–17: Ch 1, sc in 1st sc from hook and in each of next rem sc in last row of back—3 sc.

Row 18: Ch 1, sc in 1st sc from hook, ch 2 for buttonhole, sc in next sc.

Row 19: Ch 1, sc in 1st sc from hook, 2 sc in ch-2 space, sc in next sc—4 sc.

Row 20: Ch 1, sc in 1st sc from hook and in each of next rem sc—4 sc. Fasten off.

SIDES AND BOTTOM

Foundation

With WS of back facing, bottom to your left, and Yarn B, insert hook in 13th row 2nd st. Work 12 overlay chs along left side of back, from top to bottom, inserting hook in each next row 2nd st (you will now be at 1st row 2nd st). With back bottom close to you, work another 5 overlay chs along back bottom, inserting hook in each next st of 1st row (you will now be at 1st row 7th st). With back bottom to your right, work another 12 overlay chs along right side of back, from bottom to top, inserting hook in each next row 2nd st from end (you will now be at 13th row 2nd st from end). Cut yarn.

Sides and bottom

Row 1: With Yarn B, insert hook in 1st overlay ch of foundation, ch 1, sc in same st and in each of next rem overlay chs across foundation—29 sc. You now have 29 sc; 12 sc for each side, and 5 sc for the bottom. Fasten off.

FRONT

Row 1: With WS of back facing, bottom close to you, and Yarn A, insert hook in back lp of rightmost sc in last row of bottom, ch 1, sc in same lp and in each back lp of next 5 sc along bottom—5 sc.

Row 2: Ch 1, sc in 1st sc from hook, 2 sc in next sc, sc in next sc, 2 sc in next sc, sc in next sc—7 sc.

Rows 3–7: Ch 1, sc in 1st sc from hook and in each of next rem sc—7 sc.

Row 8: Ch 1, sc in 1st sc from hook, sk next sc, sc in each of next 3 sc, sk next sc, sc in next sc—5 sc.

Row 9: Ch 1, sc in 1st sc from hook and in each of next rem sc—5 sc.

Row 10: Ch 1, sc in 1st sc from hook, sk next sc, sc in next sc, sk next sc, sc in next sc—3 sc.

Row 11: Ch 1, sc in 1st sc from hook and in each of next rem sc—3 sc. Cut yarn.

ATTACHING FRONT TO SIDES

With RS of front facing, bottom to your left, and Yarn C, insert hook in 1st st at right edge in last row of front and in back lp of 1st sc in last row of right side. Ch 1, sc in same pair of sts, sc in each of next 10 pairs along right side, from top to bottom, 3 sc in back lp of next sc in last row of right side, sc in unused lps of next 5 sc along bottom, 3 sc in back lp of next sc in last row of left side, sc in 1st st at left edge in 1st row of front and in back lp of next sc in last row of left side, sc in each of next 10 pairs along left side from bottom to top. Cont and sc in each of next sc along front top. End with sl st in 1st sc. Fasten off.

CROCHETING BACK EDGES

With WS of back facing, bottom to your left, and Yarn C, insert hook in 1st st at right edge in last row of back, ch 1, sc in same st and in each of next sts along right edge of back, from top to bottom, 3 sc in corner st, sc in each of next ch of foundation chs, 3 sc in corner st, sc in each of next 1st sts along left edge of back from bottom to top. Fasten off.

CROCHETING LOOP

With RS of back facing, bottom to your right, with Yarn C, insert hook in 1st st at right edge in 1st row of loop, ch 1, sc in same st and in each of next sts along right edge of loop from bottom to top, 3 sc in corner st, sc in each of next sc in last row of loop, 3 sc in corner st, sc in each of next 1st sts along left edge of loop, from top to bottom. Fasten off.

ATTACHING BUTTON

With WS of back facing, sew button on last row of back, corresponding to buttonhole on belt loop when belt loop is folded.

INSERTING BELT

Button up belt loop and draw belt through.

this project was crocheted with

(A) 1 ball of Lion Wool-Ease Thick & Quick, 80% acrylic/20% wool, super bulky weight, approx 6oz/170g = approx 106yd/97m per ball, color 640-194

(B) 1 ball of Lion Wool-Ease Thick & Quick, 80% acrylic/20% wool, super bulky weight, approx 6oz/170g = approx 106yd/97m per ball, color 640-114

(C) 1 ball of Lion Wool-Ease Thick & Quick, 80% acrylic/20% wool, super bulky weight, approx 6oz/170g = approx 106yd/97m per ball, color 640-131

blossoming tree lingerie bag

This delicate bag is just right for storing stockings, undergarments, or your favorite scarf. The tree is crocheted using filet crochet.

EXPERIENCE LEVEL

■■■□ Intermediate

FINISHED MEASUREMENTS

14"/35.6cm wide x 17"/43.2cm high

MATERIALS AND TOOLS

Yarn A : 206yd/188m of Worsted weight yarn, organic cotton, in light beige

Yarn B : 103yd/94m of Worsted weight yarn, organic cotton, in deep brown

Yarn C : 207yd/188m of Worsted weight yarn, cotton/acrylic, in dark yellow

Yarn D : 207yd/188m of Worsted weight yarn, cotton/acrylic, in burnt orange

Size E/4 (3.5mm) crochet hook OR SIZE TO OBTAIN GAUGE

Sewing needle and matching color thread

GAUGE

With Yarn A, 8 sts and 4 rows = 2"/5cm in dc

SPECIAL STITCHES

4 DC Filet (page 17)

Picot: Ch 3, sl st in 1st ch of ch-3 (page 17)

PATTERN

4 DC Filet Tree Pattern (page 113)

instructions

FRONT (4DC FILET TREE PATTERN, PAGE 113)

Note: If you are familiar with filet crochet, follow the 4 DC Filet Tree pattern. If not, simply follow the detailed instructions below.

With Yarn A, ch 67.

Row 1: Ch 3, dc in 4th ch from hook and in each of next rem chs.

Row 2: Ch 3, dc in 1st dc and in each of next 2 dc; *(ch 2, sk 2 sts, dc in next dc). Rep from * 6 times. Dc in each of next 9 dc. Rep from * 11 times. Dc in each of next 2 dc. End with dc in 3rd ch of ch-3 of prev row.

Row 3: Ch 3, dc in 1st dc and in each of next 2 dc; *(ch 2, sk 2 sts, dc in next dc). Rep from * 12 times. Dc in each of next 6 dc. Rep from * 6 times. Dc in each of next 2 dc. End with dc in 3rd ch of ch-3 of prev row.

Row 4: Ch 3, dc in 1st dc and in each of next 2 dc; *(ch 2, sk 2 sts, dc in next dc). Rep from * 6 times. Dc in each of next 6 dc. Rep from * 12 times. Dc in each of next 2 dc. End with dc in 3rd ch of ch-3 of prev row.

Row 5: Rep row 3.

Row 6: Rep row 4.

Row 7: Rep row 3.

Row 8: Ch 3, dc in 1st dc and in each of next 2 dc; *(ch 2, sk 2 sts, dc in next dc). Rep from * 5 times. 2 dc in next ch-2 space, dc in next 4 dc. Rep from * once. ** 2 dc in next ch-2 space, dc in next dc. Rep from ** twice. Rep from * 10 times. Dc in each of next 2 dc. End with dc in 3rd ch of ch-3 of prev row.

Row 9: Ch 3, dc in 1st dc and in each of next 2 dc; *(ch 2, sk 2 sts, dc in next dc). Rep from * 8 times. **2 dc in next ch-2 space, dc in next dc. Rep from ** twice. Rep from * twice. Rep from ** once. Rep from * once. Rep from ** once. Rep from * 5 times. Dc in each of next 2 dc. End with dc in 3rd ch of ch-3 of prev row.

Row 10: Ch 3, dc in 1st dc and in each of next 2 dc; *(ch 2, sk 2 sts, dc in next dc). Rep from * 4 times. 2 dc in next ch-2 space, dc in next dc. Rep from * twice. Dc in each of next 4 dc, 2 dc in next ch-2 space, dc in next dc. Rep from * twice. 2 dc in next ch-2 space, dc in next dc. Rep from * 8 times. Dc in each of next 2 dc. End with dc in 3rd ch of ch-3 of prev row.

Row 11: Ch 3, dc in 1st dc and in each of next 2 dc; *(ch 2, sk 2 sts, dc in next dc). Rep from * 7 times. 2 dc in next ch-2 space, dc in next dc. Rep from * 3 times. Dc in each of next 6 dc. Rep from * 3 times. 2 dc in next ch-2 space, dc in next dc.

Rep from * 3 times. Dc in each of next 2 dc. End with dc in 3rd ch of ch-3 of prev row.

Row 12: Ch 3, dc in 1st dc and in each of next 2 dc; *(ch 2, sk 2 sts, dc in next dc). Rep from * 3 times. 2 dc in next ch-2 space, dc in next dc. Rep from * 3 times.

Dc in each of next 6 dc. Rep from * 11 times. Dc in each of next 2 dc. End with dc in 3rd ch of ch-3 of prev row.

Row 13: Ch 3, dc in 1st dc and in each of next 2 dc; *(ch 2, sk 2 sts, dc in next dc). Rep from * 11 times. Dc in each of next 6 dc. Rep from * 4 times. 2 dc in next ch-2 space, dc in next dc. Rep from * twice. Dc in each of next 2 dc. End with dc in 3rd ch of ch-3 of prev row.

Row 14: Ch 3, dc in 1st dc and in each of next 2 dc; *(ch 2, sk 2 sts, dc in next dc). Rep from * 5 times. **2 dc in next ch-2 space, dc in next dc. Rep from ** twice. Rep from * once. Dc in each of next 3 dc. Rep from ** once. Rep from * 10 times. Dc in each of next 2 dc. End with dc in 3rd ch of ch-3 of prev row.

Row 15: Ch 3, dc in 1st dc and in each of next 2 dc; *(ch 2, sk 2 sts, dc in next dc). Rep from * 10 times. Dc in each of next 6 dc. 2 dc in next ch-2 space, dc in next dc. Rep from * twice. 2 dc in next ch-2 space, dc in next dc. Rep from * 4 times. Dc in each of next 2 dc. End with dc in 3rd ch of ch-3 of prev row.

Row 16: Ch 3, dc in 1st dc and in each of next 2 dc; *(ch 2, sk 2 sts, dc in next dc). Rep from * 7 times. Dc in each of next 6 dc. Rep from * once. **2 dc in next ch-2 space, dc in next dc. Rep from ** twice. Rep from * 8 times. Dc in each of next 2 dc. End with dc in 3rd ch of ch-3 of prev row.

Row 17: Ch 3, dc in 1st dc and in each of next 2 dc; *(ch 2, sk 2 sts, dc in next dc). Rep from * 4 times. **2 dc in next ch-2 space, dc in next dc. Rep from ** 4 times. Dc in each of next 3 dc. Rep from * twice. Dc in each of next 6 dc. Rep from * 7 times. Dc in each of next 2 dc. End with dc in 3rd ch of ch-3 of prev row.

Row 18: Ch 3, dc in 1st dc and in each of next 2 dc; *(ch 2, sk 2 sts, dc in next dc). Rep from * 6 times. 2 dc in next ch-2 space, dc in each of next 4 dc. Rep from * once. 2 dc in next ch-2 space, dc in next dc. Rep from * 4 times. 2 dc in next ch-2 space, dc in each of next 4 dc. Rep from * once. **2 dc in next ch-2 space, dc in next dc. Rep from ** twice. Rep from * twice. Dc in each of next 2 dc. End with dc in 3rd ch of ch-3 of prev row.

Row 19: Ch 3, dc in 1st dc and in each of next 2 dc, ch 2, sk 2 sts, dc in next dc. 2 dc in next ch-2 space, dc in next dc; *(ch 2, sk 2 sts, dc in next dc). Rep from * 3 times. 2 dc in next ch-2 space, dc in next dc. Rep from * 6 times. Dc in each of next 6 dc. Rep from * 6 times. Dc in each of next 2 dc. End with dc in 3rd ch of ch-3 of prev row.

Row 20: Ch 3, dc in 1st dc and in each of next 2 dc; *(ch 2, sk 2 sts, dc in next dc). Rep from * 5 times. 2 dc in next ch-2 space, dc in each of next 7 dc. Rep from * 7 times. 2 dc in next ch-2 space, dc in next dc. Rep from * 4 times. Dc in each of next 2 dc. End with dc in 3rd ch of ch-3 of prev row.

Row 21: Ch 3, dc in 1st dc and in each of next 2 dc; *(ch 2, sk 2 sts, dc in next dc). Rep from * 3 times. 2 dc in next ch-2 space, dc in next dc. Rep from * 8 times. Dc in each of next 3 dc. Rep from * once. Dc in each of next 3 dc. 2 dc in next ch-2 space, dc in next dc. Rep from * 4 times. Dc in each of next 2 dc. End with dc in 3rd ch of ch-3 of prev row.

Row 22: Ch 3, dc in 1st dc and in each of next 2 dc; *(ch

2, sk 2 sts, dc in next dc). Rep from * 5 times. Dc in each of next 3 dc. Rep from * once. Dc in each of next 3 dc. Rep from * 12 times. Dc in each of next 2 dc. End with dc in 3rd ch of ch-3 of prev row.

Row 23: Ch 3, dc in 1st dc and in each of next 2 dc; *(ch 2, sk 2 sts, dc in next dc). Rep from * 12 times. Dc in each of next 3 dc. Rep from * once. Dc in each of next 3 dc. 2 dc in next ch-2 space, dc in next dc. Rep from * 4 times. Dc in each of next 2 dc. End with dc in 3rd ch of ch-3 of prev row.

Row 24: Ch 3, dc in 1st dc and in each of next 2 dc; *(ch 2, sk 2 sts, dc in next dc). Rep from * 3 times. 2 dc in next ch-2 space, dc in next dc. Rep from * once. Dc in each of next 3 dc. Rep from * once. Dc in each of next 3 dc. 2 dc in next ch-2 space, dc in next dc. Rep from * 11 times. Dc in each of next 2 dc. End with dc in 3rd ch of ch-3 of prev row.

Dc in each of next 2 dc. End with dc in 3rd ch of ch-3 of prev row.

Row 28: Ch 3, dc in 1st dc and in each of next 2 dc; *(ch 2, sk 2 sts, dc in next dc). Rep from * 3 times. 2 dc in next ch-2 space, dc in each of next 3 dc. Rep from * 6 times. 2 dc in next ch-2 space, dc in next dc. Rep from * 8 times. Dc in each of next 2 dc. End with dc in 3rd ch of ch-3 of prev row.

Row 29: Ch 3, dc in 1st dc and in each of next 2 dc; *(ch 2, sk 2 sts, dc in next dc). Rep from * 7 times. 2 dc in next ch-2 space, dc in next dc. Rep from * once. 2 dc in next ch-2 space, dc in next dc. Rep from * 6 times. Dc in each of next 3 dc. 2 dc in next ch-2 space, dc in next dc. Rep from * twice. Dc in each of next 2 dc. End with dc in 3rd ch of ch-3 of prev row.

Row 30: Ch 3, dc in 1st dc and in each of next 2 dc; *(ch 2, sk 2 sts, dc in next dc). Rep from * 4 times. 2 dc in next ch-2 space, dc in next dc. Rep from * 15 times. Dc in each of next 2 dc. End with dc in 3rd ch of ch-3 of prev row.

Row 31: Ch 3, dc in 1st dc and in each of next 2 dc; *(ch 2, sk 2 sts, dc in next dc). Rep from * 20 times. Dc in each of next 2 dc. End with dc in 3rd ch of ch-3 of prev row.

Row 32: Ch 3, dc in 1st dc and in each of next 2 dc; ** 2 dc in next ch-2 space, dc in next dc. Rep from ** 20 times. Dc in each of next 2 dc. End with dc in 3rd ch of ch-3 of prev row. Fasten off.

- - - - - - - - - - - - - - - - - - -

BACK

With Yarn A, ch 67.

Row 1: Ch 3, dc in 4th ch from hook and in each of next rem chs.

Rows 2–4: Ch 3, dc in 1st dc and in each of next 2 dc; *(ch 2, sk 2 sts, dc in next dc). Rep from * 20 times. Dc in each of next 2 dc. End with dc in 3rd ch of ch-3 of prev row.

Row 5: Ch 3, dc in 1st dc and in each of next 2 dc; *(ch 2, sk 2 sts, dc in next dc). Rep from * 3 times. Don't cut yarn. Join Yarn B, **2 dc in next ch-2 space, dc in next dc.

Row 25: Ch 3, dc in 1st dc and in each of next 2 dc; *(ch 2, sk 2 sts, dc in next dc). Rep from * 11 times. Dc in each of next 6 dc. Rep from * once. Dc in each of next 3 dc. Rep from * once. Dc in each of next 3 dc. 2 dc in next ch-2 space, dc in next dc. Rep from * twice. Dc in each of next 2 dc. End with dc in 3rd ch of ch-3 of prev row.

Row 26: Ch 3, dc in 1st dc and in each of next 2 dc, ch 2, sk 2 sts, dc in next dc. 2 dc in next ch-2 space, dc in next dc; *(ch 2, sk 2 sts, dc in next dc). Rep from * 3 times. Dc in each of next 3 dc. Rep from * once. Dc in each of next 3 dc. Rep from * once. 2 dc in next ch-2 space, dc in next dc. Rep from * 10 times. Dc in each of next 2 dc. End with dc in 3rd ch of ch-3 of prev row.

Row 27: Ch 3, dc in 1st dc and in each of next 2 dc; *(ch 2, sk 2 sts, dc in next dc). Rep from * 8 times. ** 2 dc in next ch-2 space, dc in next dc. Rep from ** twice. Rep from * once. Rep from ** once. Rep from * twice. Dc in each of next 3 dc. Rep from ** once. Rep from * 4 times.

Rep from ** 13 times. 2 dc in next ch-2 space. Don't cut yarn. Join Yarn A (use other ball), dc in next dc. Rep from * 3 times. Dc in each of next 2 dc. End with dc in 3rd ch of ch-3 of prev row.

Rows 6–11: Ch 3, dc in 1st dc and in each of next 2 dc; *(ch 2, sk 2 sts, dc in next dc). Rep from * 3 times. Don't cut yarn. With Yarn B, dc in each of next 41 dc. Don't cut yarn. With Yarn A, dc in next dc. Rep from * 3 times. Dc in each of next 2 dc. End with dc in 3rd ch of ch-3 of prev row.

Rows 12–21: Ch 3, dc in 1st dc and in each of next 2 dc; *(ch 2, sk 2 sts, dc in next dc). Rep from * 3 times. Don't cut yarn. With Yarn B, dc in each of next 15 dc. Rep from * 4 times. Dc in each of next 14 dc. Don't cut yarn. With Yarn A, dc in next dc. Rep from * 3 times. Dc in each of next 2 dc. End with dc in 3rd ch of ch-3 of prev row.

Row 22: Ch 3, dc in 1st dc and in each of next 2 dc; *(ch 2, sk 2 sts, dc in next dc). Rep from * 3 times. Don't cut yarn. With Yarn B, dc in each of next 15 dc. **2 dc in next ch-2 space, dc in next dc. Rep from ** 4 times. Dc in each of next 14 dc. Don't cut yarn. With Yarn A, dc in next dc. Rep from * 3 times. Dc in each of next 2 dc. End with dc in 3rd ch of ch-3 of prev row.

Rows 23–28: Ch 3, dc in 1st dc and in each of next 2 dc; *(ch 2, sk 2 sts, dc in next dc). Rep from * 3 times. Cut Yarn A. With Yarn B, dc in each of next 41 dc. Cut Yarn B. With Yarn A, dc in next dc. Rep from * 3 times. Dc in each of next 2 dc. End with dc in 3rd ch of ch-3 of prev row.

Rows 29 -31: Rep rows 2 – 4.

Row 32: Ch 3, dc in 1st dc and in each of next 2 dc; **2 dc in next ch-2 space, dc in next dc. Rep from ** 20 times. Dc in each of next 2 dc. End with dc in 3rd ch of ch-3 of prev row. Fasten off.

CROCHETING FRONT AND BACK EDGES

With RS of front (back) facing, bottom close to you, and Yarn D, insert hook in rightmost dc at front (back) top, ch 1, 3 sc in same dc, sc in each of next dc along front (back) top, 3 sc in leftmost dc at front (back) top; cont along one side, from top to bottom, with 3 sc in edge st of each row; 3 sc in rightmost ch of foundation chs at front (back) bottom, sc in each of next ch of foundation chs along front (back) bottom, 3 sc in leftmost ch at front (back) bottom; cont along other side, from bottom to top, with 3 sc in edge st of each row. Join with sl st in 1st sc. Fasten off.

FLOWER (MAKE 12: 4 START WITH YARN D; 8 START WITH YARN C)

With Yarn C (Yarn D), ch 5, join with sl st in 1st ch to form a ring.

Rnd 1: Ch 1, 9 sc in ring. Join with sl st in 1st sc.

Rnd 2: Join Yarn D (Yarn C), picot, sk joining st; *sl st in next sc, picot, sk next sc. Rep from * 8 times. Join with sl st in 1st ch from beg of rnd. Fasten off.

ATTACHING FLOWERS TO FRONT

Place WS of flowers on RS bag front at places indicated on pattern. Sew on flower centers with a few hidden sts.

ATTACHING BACK TO FRONT

Place front and back with WS tog.

With RS of front facing, bottom to your left, and Yarn D, insert hook about 4½"/11.4cm from top in front lp of edge sc of front, and back lp of corresponding sc at back, *picot, sk next sc at front and back, sl st in front lp of next sc at front and in back lp of next sc at back. Rep from * along side, from top to bottom, along bottom, and up other side, from bottom to top, until you are about 4½"/11.4cm from top. Cont to work around front to form an opening. *Picot, sk next sc at front, sl st in front lp of next sc at front. Rep from * along rem 4½"/11.4cm of side, along top, and 4½"/11.4cm along other side. Join with sl st in 1st ch from beg of rnd. Fasten off.

With WS of back facing, bottom to your right, and Yarn

D, insert hook in back lp of 1st sc of opening, *picot, sk next sc, sl st in back lp of next sc. Rep from * along rem 4½"/11.4cm of side, along top, and 4½"/11.4cm along other side. Join with sl st in front lp of last rnd joining st and in back lp of same st. Join with sl st in 1st ch from beg of rnd. Fasten off.

INSIDE BORDER (REP TWICE)

With WS of front (back) facing, bottom away, and Yarn C, insert hook in rightmost unused lp at top corner, ch 3, dc in next unused lp, and in each rem unused lp along top. Fasten off.

With bag open and WS facing, front to your right (left), and Yarn C, insert hook into 3rd unused lp from top of front (back) at side of opening, ch 3, dc in next unused lp, and in each rem unused lp until 3rd unused lp of back (front). Fasten off.

Sew tog adjacent border ends to connect corners.

RIBBON (MAKE 6)

With RS of front (back) facing, bottom close to you, and 2 strands of Yarn C, insert hook in rightmost picot at front (back) top and ch 50. Cut yarn and tie ends. Don't hide tails of loose ribbon end.

Follow same instruction for making other ribbons, inserting hook in leftmost picot and in middle picot at front (back) top.

CLOVER (MAKE 6)

With Yarn D, insert hook into 2nd ch at ribbon end, *picot, sc in same ch of ribbon. Rep from * twice in front lp of ch st and once in back lp of same ch. End with sl st in 1st ch from beg rnd. Cut yarn and tie ends. Don't hide tails. With Yarn C, insert hook into 2nd ch at other end of ribbon and make another clover.

HANDLE

With Yarn D, ch 50.

Row 1: Ch 3, dc in 4th ch from hook and in each of next rem chs—50 dc. Fasten off.

SEWING ON HANDLE

With RS of back facing, bottom close to you, and Yarn D, position each end of handle 4½"/11.4cm from each side and immediately above open mesh. Sew on handle at edges and just below crocheted top.

this project was crocheted with

(A) 2 balls of Lion Nature's Choice Organic Cotton, 100% organic cotton, worsted weight, 3oz/85g = approx 103yd/94m per ball, color #480-099

(B) 1 ball of Lion Nature's Choice Organic Cotton, 100% organic cotton, worsted weight, 3oz/85g = approx 103yd/94m per ball, color #480-124

(C) 1 ball of Lion Cotton-Ease, 50% cotton/50% acrylic, worsted weight, 3.5oz/100g = approx 207yd/188m per ball, color #830-186

(D) 1 ball of Lion Cotton-Ease, 50% cotton/50% acrylic, worsted weight, 3.5oz/100g = approx 207yd/188m per ball, color #830-134

(E) 1 ball of Lion Cotton-Ease, 50% cotton/50% acrylic, worsted weight, 3.5oz/100g = approx 207yd/188m per ball, color #830-134

4 DC filet tree pattern

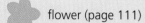 open mesh (page 17)

solid mesh (page 17)

flower (page 111)

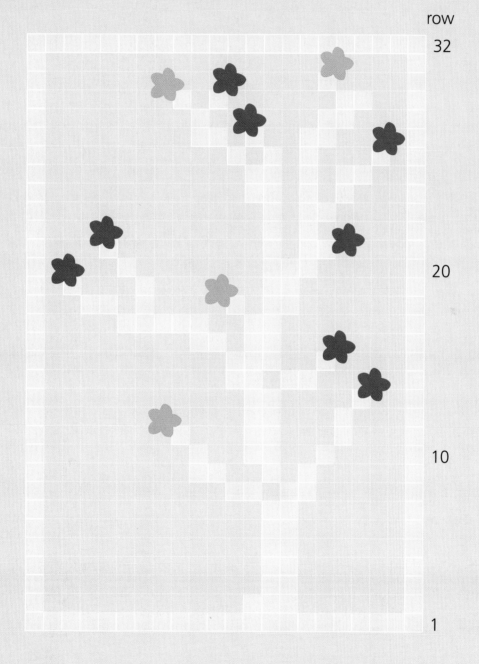

row

32

20

10

1

Note: Begin each row with ch 3. End each row with dc in 3rd ch of ch-3 of prev row.

decorated shoe sack

Bring along one or two extra pairs of shoes with this attractive hemp sack. In winter, it's perfect for storing shoes on days when you wear boots. In summer, use it to carry along flip flops or sandals.

EXPERIENCE LEVEL

 Intermediate

FINISHED MEASUREMENTS

5½"/14cm in diameter x 18½"/47cm high

MATERIALS AND TOOLS

Yarn A **MEDIUM 4**: 103yd/94m of Worsted weight yarn, organic cotton, in medium green

Yarn B **MEDIUM 4**: 103yd/94m of Worsted weight yarn, organic cotton, in light brown

Yarn C **MEDIUM 4**: 103yd/94m of Worsted weight yarn, organic cotton, in light beige

Yarn D **MEDIUM 4**: 103yd/94m of Worsted weight yarn, organic cotton, in deep brown

Yarn E **MEDIUM 4**: 103yd/94m of Worsted weight yarn, organic cotton, in white

Yarn F **MEDIUM 4**: 207yd/188m of Worsted weight yarn, cotton/acrylic, in dark yellow

Yarn G **MEDIUM 4**: 207yd/188m of Worsted weight yarn, cotton/acrylic, in burnt orange

Size E/4 (3.5mm) crochet hook OR SIZE TO OBTAIN GAUGE

Natural hemp sack cloth: Two rectangles, each 9½"/24.1cm wide x 21"/53.3cm long; one circle, 6½"/16.5cm diameter

Straight pins

Sewing needle and color thread

One piece of orange bias tape, 1"/2.5cm wide x 80"/203.2cm long

Safety pin

Two pieces of ⁵⁄₃₂"/4mm natural beige hemp rope, 50"/127cm long

GAUGE

With Yarn A, 8 sts and 8 rows = 2"/5cm in sc

SPECIAL STITCHES

Picot: Ch 3, sl st in 1st ch of ch-3 (page 17)

Popcorn Stitch (Popcorn): 3 dc in next st, remove hook from lp and insert in ch-3 space, insert into dropped st and draw it through, ch 3 (page 16)

instructions

DECORATIVE SQUARES

Note: Same instructions apply to each square, but follow a different color diagram.

Square 1

With Yarn A, ch 5, join with sl st in 1st ch to form a ring.

Rnd 1: Ch 1, 6 sc in ring. Join with sl st in 1st sc. Cut yarn.

Rnd 2: Join Yarn E, ch 4, dc in same sc as joining, ch 1; *(dc, ch 1, dc) all in next sc, ch 1. Rep from * 5 times. Join with sl st in 3rd ch of beg ch-4—12 dc, including 1st chs. Cut yarn.

Rnd 3: Join Yarn B, sl st into space between ch-4 and 1st dc of prev rnd and ch 3, 2 dc in same ch-1 space. Remove hook from lp and insert in space between ch-3 and 1st dc, insert into dropped lp and draw it through, ch 3 (this makes 1st Popcorn); * Popcorn in next ch-1 space. Rep from * 11 times—12 Popcorns. Cut yarn.

Rnd 4: Join Yarn D, sl st into space between 1st and 2nd Popcorns of prev rnd and ch 4; (dc, ch 1, dc) all in next ch-3 space, ch 4, (dc, ch 1, dc) all in next ch-3 space, ch 2; *sc in next ch-3 space, ch 2, (dc, ch 1, dc) all in next ch-3 space, ch 4, (dc, ch 1, dc) all in next ch-3 space, ch 2. Rep from * 3 times. Join with sl st in 2nd ch of beg ch-4.

Rnd 5: Ch 2, 2 sc into space between ch-4 and 1st dc of prev rnd, sc in next dc, sc in next ch-1 space, sc in next dc, 5 sc in next ch-4 space, sc in next dc, sc in next ch-1 space, sc in next dc, 2 sc in next ch-2 space; *sc in next sc, 2 sc in next ch-2 space, sc in next dc, sc in next ch-1 space, sc in next dc, 5 sc in next ch-4 space, sc in next dc, sc in next ch-1 space sc in next dc, 2 sc in next ch-2 space. Rep from * 3 times. Join with sl st in 2nd ch of beg ch-2. Cut yarn.

Rnd 6: Join Yarn E, ch 2, sc in each of next 7 sc, 3 sc in next sc (corner st); *sc in each of next 15 sc, 3 sc in next sc (corner st). Rep from * 3 times. Sc in each of next 7 sc. Join with sl st in 2nd ch of beg ch-2. Fasten off.

Square 2

Ring and Rnd 1: Yarn A; Rnd 2: Yarn D; Rnd 3: Yarn C; Rnds 4–5: Yarn B; Rnd 6: Yarn D.

Square 3

Ring and Rnd 1: Yarn B; Rnd 2: Yarn A; Rnd 3: Yarn E; Rnds 4–5: Yarn C; Rnd 6: Yarn A

Square 4

Ring and Rnd 1: Yarn C; Rnd 2: Yarn B; Rnd 3: Yarn A; Rnds 4–5: Yarn D; Rnd 6: Yarn B.

HEMP SACK CLOTH PREPARATION

Note: Hemp fabric tends to fray at the edges, so seams are sewn along edges to prevent fraying.

Make a ½"/1.3cm fold all around each rectangle, and around circle, and sew seam ¼"/0.6cm from fold. Side with fold is WS.

RECTANGLE 1

Drawstring tracks

Row 1: With RS of rectangle facing, shorter side close to you, and Yarn A, insert hook in fabric 1½"/3.8cm left of right edge and 5½"/14cm from top. Work 35 overlay chs evenly along top, or until you are 1½"/3.8cm right of left edge. Cut yarn.

Note: Begin every row at right side of rectangle.

Row 2: With Yarn B, insert hook in back lp of 1st overlay ch, ch 3, dc in back lp of next overlay ch and in each of next rem overlay chs. Fasten off.

Row 3: With Yarn A, insert hook in 3rd ch of beg ch-3 and in corresponding place in fabric, and work overlay chs along this row, inserting hook in each dc st and its corresponding place in fabric. Fasten off.

Rows 4 and 5: Rep rows 2 and 3.

Crocheting track edges

With RS of hemp rectangle facing, top away (close), and Yarn F, insert hook in back lp of 1st (last) overlay ch of last (1st) row. *Picot, sk next st, sl st in back lp of next st. Rep from * to last (1st) overlay ch. Fasten off.

Attaching squares

Place RS of hemp rectangle and WS of Square 4 tog, so that top of square is 2"/5cm below lower drawstring track and in middle, and pin. Place Square 3 2"/5cm below 1st square, and pin.

(Rep twice)

With RS of rectangle facing, top away from you, and Yarn D, insert hook in rightmost front lp of sc at top of Square 4 (Square 3). Work overlay chs in front lp of each sc around square edge and in corresponding place in fabric. Join with sl st in 1st overlay ch.

Crocheting square edge (rep twice)

With Yarn F, insert hook in back lp of joining st of attaching rnd. Picot, sk next st, *sl st in back lp of next st, picot, sk next st. Rep from * all around edge. Join with sl st in 1st ch from beg of rnd. Fasten off

RECTANGLE 2

Note: Follow same instruction as for Rectangle 1, using the following yarns.

Drawstring tracks

Rows 1, 3, and 5: Yarn A

Rows 2 and 4: Yarn D.

Crocheted track edges: Yarn G

Attaching squares

Yarn A to attach Square 2 at top and Square 1 at bottom.

Crocheting square edge

Yarn G

SEWING SACK TOGETHER

With RS of rectangles tog, place side edges tog. Cut two 20"/50.8cm pieces of bias tape, fold evenly over each side edges, and pin. Sew along sides, ½"/1.3cm from edge, to make bound seams.

With WS of body and side of circle with folded edge facing, place bottom of body and circle tog. Cut a 20"/50.8cm piece of bias tape, fold evenly over bottom edge and edge of circle, and pin. Sew all around, ½"/1.3cm from edge, to make a bound seam.

With WS of body facing, make a 1½"/3.8cm fold at top of body. Place rem 20"/50.8cm piece of bias tape all around top of body, ½"/1.3cm from folded edge and pin. Make sure bias tape covers edge of fabric. Sew seams along top and bottom of bias tape, all around body.

INSERTING DRAWSTRING (REP TWICE)

Attach safety pin to one end of drawstring. With RS of Rectangle 1 (Rectangle 2) facing and top away, insert end of drawstring with safety pin into right opening of lower (upper) drawstring track and draw through track and out through left opening. Turn sack over, with RS of Rectangle 2 (Rectangle 1) facing, insert end into right opening of lower (upper) track. Draw through and out left opening until ends are even. Tie ends together with an overhand knot.

this project was crocheted with

(A) 1 ball of Lion Nature's Choice Organic Cotton, 100% organic cotton, worsted weight, 3oz/85g = approx 103yd/94m per ball, color #480-170

(B) 1 ball of Lion Nature's Choice Organic Cotton, 100% organic cotton, worsted weight, 3oz/85g = approx 103yd/94m per ball, color #480-124

(C) 1 ball of Lion Nature's Choice Organic Cotton, 100% organic cotton, worsted weight, 3oz/85g = approx 103yd/94m per ball, color #480-099

(D) 1 ball of Lion Nature's Choice Organic Cotton, 100% organic cotton, worsted weight, 3oz/85g = approx 103yd/94m per ball, color #480-125

(E) 1 ball of Lion Nature's Choice Organic Cotton, 100% organic cotton, worsted weight, 3oz/85g = approx 103yd/94m per ball, color #480-098

(F) 1 ball of Lion Cotton-Ease, 50% cotton/50% acrylic, worsted weight, 3.5oz/100g = approx 207yd/188m per ball, color #830-186

(G) 1 ball of Lion Cotton-Ease, 50% cotton/50% acrylic, worsted weight, 3.5oz/100g = approx 207yd/188m per ball, color #830-134

Fabric: HempBasics Natural Hemp Sack Cloth

Rope: HempBasics ⁵⁄₃₂"/4mm Natural Beige Hemp Rope

traveler's make-up container

Store lipstick, eyeliner, and other essentials in this sturdy bag. It matches the Genie's Jewelry Box (page 124) and features a clover-tipped drawstring for closing.

EXPERIENCE LEVEL

◼◼◻◻ Easy

FINISHED MEASUREMENTS

5½"/14cm in diameter x 18½"/47cm high

MATERIALS AND TOOLS

Yarn A : 103yd/94m of Worsted weight yarn, organic cotton, in light brown

Yarn B : 103yd/94m of Worsted weight yarn, organic cotton, in deep brown

Yarn C : 207yd/188m of Worsted weight yarn, cotton/acrylic, in dark olive green

Yarn D : 207yd/188m of Worsted weight yarn, cotton/acrylic, in dark yellow

Yarn E : 207yd/188m of Worsted weight yarn, cotton/acrylic, in burnt orange

Size E/4 (3.5mm) crochet hook OR SIZE TO OBTAIN GAUGE

GAUGE

With Yarn A, 8 sts and 8 rows = 2"/5cm in sc

SPECIAL STITCHES

Picot: Ch 3, sl st in 1st ch of ch-3 (page 17)

instructions

OVAL BOTTOM

With Yarn B, ch 21.

Rnd 1: Sc in the 2nd ch from hook, sc in each of next 19 chs, ch 1. Don't turn. Work along bottom side of foundation chs, sc in unused lps of next 20 chs, ch 1. Join with sl st in 1st sc—40 sc.

Rnd 2: Ch 1, sc in same sc as joining and in each of next 19 sc, 5 sc in next ch-1 space, sc in each of next 20 sc, 5 sc in next ch-1 space. Join with sl st in 1st sc—50 sc.

Rnd 3: Ch 1, sc in same sc as joining and in each of next 19 sc, 2 sc in each of next 5 sc, sc in each of next 20 sc, 2 sc in each of next 5 sc. Join with sl st in 1st sc—60 sc.

Rnd 4: Ch 1, sc in 1st sc from hook and in each of next rem sc. Join with sl st in 1st sc—60 sc.

Rnd 5: Ch 1, sc in same sc as joining and in each of next 19 sc, 2 sc in next sc, sc in each of next 8 sc, 2 sc in next sc, sc in each of next 20 sc, 2 sc in next sc, sc in each of next 8 sc, 2 sc in next sc. Join with sl st in 1st sc—64 sc.

Rnd 6: Ch 1, sc in same sc as joining and in each of next 19 sc, 2 sc in next sc, sc in each of next 10 sc, 2 sc in next sc, sc in each of next 20 sc, 2 sc in next sc, sc in each of next 10 sc, 2 sc in next sc. Join with sl st in 1st sc—68 sc.

Rnd 7: Ch 1, sc in same sc as joining and in each of next rem sc. Join with sl st in 1st sc—68 sc. Cut yarn.

BODY

Rnds 1–8: Join Yarn A, ch 1, sc in same sc as joining and in each of next rem sc. Join with sl st in 1st sc—68 sc.

Rnd 9: Ch 1, sc in same sc as joining and in each of next 19 sc, sk next sc, sc in each of next 12 sc, sk next sc, sc in each of next 20 sc, sk next sc, sc in each of next 12 sc, sk next sc. Join with sl st in 1st sc—64 sc.

Rnd 10: Ch 1, sc in same sc as joining and in each of next 19 sc, sk next sc, sc in each of next 10 sc, sk next sc, sc in each of next 20 sc, sk next sc, sc in each of next 10 sc, sk next sc. Join with sl st in 1st sc—60 sc.

Rnd 11: Ch 1, sc same sc as joining and in each of next rem sc. Join with sl st in 1st sc—60 sc.

Rnd 12: Ch 1, inserting hook in front lp only, sc in same sc as joining and in each rem sc. Join with sl st in front lp of 1st sc—60 sc. Cut yarn.

Rnd 13: Join Yarn B, ch 1, sc in same sc as joining and in each of next 19 sc, sk next sc, sc in each of next 8 sc, sk next sc, sc in each of next 20 sc, sk next sc, sc in each of next 8 sc, sk next sc. Join with sl st in 1st sc—56 sc.

Rnd 14: Ch 1, sc same sc as joining and in each of next rem sc. Join with sl st in 1st sc—56 sc.

Rnd 15: Join Yarn D, picot, sk joining st; *sl st in next sc, picot, sk next sc. Rep from * 27 times. Join with sl st in 1st ch from beg of rnd. Fasten off.

FAUX SACK

Rnd 1: With RS of body facing, bottom close to you, and Yarn C, insert hook in back lp of joining st in 12th rnd of body, ch 1, sc in same st, inserting hook in back lp only sc in each rem sc. Join with sl st in 1st sc—60 sc.

Rnds 2–7: Ch 1, inserting hook in back lp only, sc in same sc as joining and in each rem sc. Join with sl st in back lp of 1st sc—60 sc.

Rnd 8: Ch 3, sk joining st, hdc in next sc, ch 1, *sk next sc, hdc in next sc, ch 1. Rep from * 29 times. Join with sl st in 2nd ch of beg ch-3.

Rnd 9: Ch 1, 2 sc in 1st ch-2 space of prev rnd and in each of next rem ch-2 spaces. Join with sl st in 1st sc—60 sc. Cut yarn.

Rnd 10: Join Yarn E, picot, sk joining st; *sl st in next sc, picot, sk next sc. Rep from * 29 times. Join with sl st in 1st ch from beg of rnd. Fasten off.

RIBBON

With 2 strands of Yarn C, ch 100. Cut yarn and tie ends. Don't hide tails.

Insert ribbon into 8th rnd of faux sack at front middle into space between

2 hdc sts. Draw ribbon around by weaving it through spaces between 2 hdc sts. Pull out at front middle.

CLOVERS (MAKE 2)

With Yarn D, insert hook into 2nd ch at one ribbon end, *picot, sc in same ch of ribbon. Rep from * twice in front lp of ch st and 1 more time in back lp of same ch. End with sl st in 1st ch from beg rnd. Cut yarn and tie ends. Don't hide tails.

this project was crocheted with

(A) 1 ball of Lion Nature's Choice Organic Cotton, 100% organic cotton, worsted weight, 3oz/85g = approx 103yd/94m per ball, color #480-124

(B) 1 ball of Lion Nature's Choice Organic Cotton, 100% organic cotton, worsted weight, 3oz/85g = approx 103yd/94m per ball, color #480-125

(C) 1 ball of Lion Cotton-Ease, 50% cotton/50% acrylic, worsted weight, 3.5oz/100g = approx 207yd/188m per ball, color #830-132

(D) 1 ball of Lion Cotton-Ease, 50% cotton/50% acrylic, worsted weight, 3.5oz/100g = approx 207yd/188m per ball, color #830-186

(E) 1 ball of Lion Cotton-Ease, 50% cotton/50% acrylic, worsted weight, 3.5oz/100g = approx 207yd/188m per ball, color #830-134

genie's jewelry box

Reminiscent of Aladdin's magical lamp, this soft box is perfect for storing your most precious jewelry. It's an ideal size for traveling, too.

EXPERIENCE LEVEL

 Easy

FINISHED MEASUREMENTS

5½"/14cm diameter at bottom x 4½"/11.4cm high (with lid)

MATERIALS AND TOOLS

Yarn A **MEDIUM 4** : 103yd/94m of Worsted weight yarn, organic cotton, in medium green

Yarn B **MEDIUM 4** : 103yd/94m of Worsted weight yarn, organic cotton, in light brown

Yarn C **MEDIUM 4** : 207yd/188m of Worsted weight yarn, cotton/acrylic, in dark yellow

Yarn D **MEDIUM 4** : 207yd/188m of Worsted weight yarn, cotton/acrylic, in dark olive green

Size E/4 (3.5mm) crochet hook OR SIZE TO OBTAIN GAUGE

Sewing needle and thread

Scissors

GAUGE

With Yarn A, 8 sts and 8 rows = 2"/5cm in sc

SPECIAL STITCHES

Picot: Ch 3, sl st in 1st ch of ch-3 (page 17)

instructions

ROUND BOTTOM

With Yarn B, ch 5, join with sl st in 1st ch to form a ring.

Rnd 1: Ch 1, 8 sc in ring. Join with sl st in 1st sc.

Rnd 2: Ch 1, 2 sc in same sc as joining and in each rem sc. Join with sl st in 1st sc—16 sc.

Rnd 3: Ch 1, sc in same sc as joining, 2 sc in next sc, *sc in next sc, 2 sc in next sc. Rep from * 7 times. Join with sl st in 1st sc—24 sc.

Rnd 4: Ch 1, sc in same sc as joining and in next sc, 2 sc in next sc, *sc in each of next 2 sc, 2 sc in next sc. Rep from * 7 times. Join with sl st in 1st sc—32 sc.

Rnd 5: Ch 1, sc in same sc as joining and in each of next 2 sc, 2 sc in next sc, *sc in each of next 3 sc, 2 sc in next sc. Rep from * 7 times. Join with sl st in 1st sc—40 sc.

Rnd 6: Ch 1, sc in same sc as joining and in each of next 3 sc, 2 sc in next sc, *sc in each of next 4 sc, 2 sc in next sc. Rep from * 7 times. Join with sl st in 1st sc—48 sc.

Rnd 7: Ch 1, sc in same sc as joining and in each of next 4 sc, 2 sc in next sc, *sc in each of next 5 sc, 2 sc in next sc. Rep from * 7 times. Join with sl st in 1st sc—56 sc.

Rnd 8: Ch 1, sc in same sc as joining and in each rem sc. Join with sl st in 1st sc. Cut yarn.

BODY

Rnd 1: Join Yarn A, ch 1, sc in same sc as joining and in each of next 5 sc, 2 sc in next sc, *sc in each of next 6 sc, 2 sc in next sc. Rep from * 7 times. Join with sl st in 1st sc—64 sc.

Rnds 2–7: Ch 1, sc in same sc as joining and in each rem sc. Join with sl st in 1st sc.

Rnd 8: Ch 1, sc in same sc as joining and in each of next 6 sc, sk next sc, *sc in each of next 7 sc, sk next sc. Rep from * 7 times. Join with sl st in 1st sc—56 sc.

Rnd 9: Ch 1, sc in same sc as joining and in each of next 5 sc, sk next sc, *sc in each of next 6 sc, sk next sc. Rep from * 7 times. Join with sl st in 1st sc—48 sc.

Rnd 10: Ch 1, sc in same sc as joining and in each of next 4 sc, sk next sc, *sc in each of next 5 sc, sk next sc. Rep from * 7 times. Join with sl st in 1st sc—40 sc. Cut yarn.

Rnds 11–16: Join Yarn C, ch 1, inserting hook in back lp only, sc in same sc as joining and in each rem sc. Join with sl st in back lp of 1st sc.

Rnd 17: Ch 3, sk joining st, hdc in next sc, ch 1, *sk next sc, hdc in next sc, ch 1. Rep from * 19 times. Join with sl st in 2nd ch of beg ch-3.

Rnd 18: Ch 1, 2 sc in 1st ch-2 space of prev rnd and in each of next rem ch-2 spaces. Join with sl st in 1st sc—40 sc. Fasten off.

LID

With Yarn B, ch 5, join with sl st in 1st ch to form a ring.

Rnd 1: Ch 1, 8 sc in ring. Join with sl st in 1st sc.

Rnds 2–3: Ch 1, sc in same sc as joining and in each rem sc. Join with sl st in 1st sc—8 sc.

Rnd 4: Ch 1, 2 sc in same sc as joining and in each rem sc. Join with sl st in 1st sc—16 sc. Cut yarn.

Rnds 5–6: Join Yarn A, ch 1, sc in same sc as joining and in each rem sc. Join with sl st in 1st sc—16 sc.

Rnd 7: Ch 1, sc in same sc as joining and in each of next 2 sc, 2 sc in next sc, *sc in each of next 3 sc, 2 sc in next sc. Rep from * 3 times. Join with sl st in 1st sc—20 sc.

Rnd 8: Ch 1, sc in same sc as joining and in each of next 3 sc, 2 sc in next sc, *sc in each of next 4 sc, 2 sc in next sc. Rep from * 3 times. Join with sl st in 1st sc—24 sc.

Rnd 9: Ch 1, sc in same sc as joining and in each of next 4 sc, 2 sc in next sc, *sc in each of next 5 sc, 2 sc in next sc. Rep from * 3 times. Join with sl st in 1st sc—28 sc.

Rnd 10: Ch 1, sc in same sc as joining and in each of next 5 sc, 2 sc in next sc, *sc in each of next 6 sc, 2 sc in next sc. Rep from * 3 times. Join with sl st in 1st sc—32 sc.

Rnd 11: Ch 1, sc in same sc as joining and in each of next 6 sc, 2 sc in next sc, *sc in each of next 7 sc, 2 sc in next sc. Rep from * 3 times. Join with sl st in 1st sc—36 sc. Cut yarn.

Rnd 12: Join Yarn B, ch 1, sc in same sc as joining and in each of next 7 sc, 2 sc in next sc, *sc in each of next 8 sc, 2 sc in next sc. Rep from * 3 times. Join with sl st in 1st sc—40 sc. Cut yarn.

Rnd 13: Join Yarn C, ch 3, sl st in 1st ch of ch-3, sk joining st, sl st in next sc, *picot, sk next sc, sl st in next sc. Rep from * 19 times. Join with sl st in 1st ch from beg of rnd. Fasten off.

RIBBON

With 2 strands of Yarn D, ch 70. Cut yarn and tie ends. Don't hide tails.

Insert ribbon into 17th round of body at front middle, in space between 2 hdc sts (10th space from joining st of this rnd). Draw ribbon around by weaving it through spaces between 2 hdc sts. Pull out at front middle.

CLOVER

With Yarn C, insert hook into 2nd ch at one ribbon end, *picot, sc in same ch of ribbon. Rep from * twice in front lp of ch st and 1 more time in back lp of same ch. End with sl st in 1st ch from beg rnd. Cut yarn and tie ends. Don't hide tails.

With Yarn C, insert hook into 2nd ch at other ribbon end and make another clover.

ATTACHING CLOVER

Place clover with its last rnd joining st matching same st at 11th rnd of body.

Sew clover onto bag body with a few simple stitches.

this project was crocheted with

(A) 1 ball of Lion Nature's Choice Organic Cotton, 100% organic cotton, worsted weight, 3oz/85g = approx 103yd/94m per ball, color #480-170

(B) 1 ball of Lion Nature's Choice Organic Cotton, 100% organic cotton, worsted weight, 3oz/85g = approx 103yd/94m per ball, color #480-124

(C) 1 ball of Lion Cotton-Ease, 50% cotton/50% acrylic, worsted weight, 3.5oz/100g = approx 207yd/188m per ball, color #830-186

(D) 1 ball of Lion Cotton-Ease, 50% cotton/50% acrylic, worsted weight, 3.5oz/100g = approx 207yd/188m per ball, color #830-132

index